To Fold the Evening Star: New & Selected Poems

Ian McMillan is among the UK's most popular living poets. His books of poems, stories, and non-fiction have drawn audiences for almost forty years. Born in Barnsley in 1956, Ian became a freelance writer, performer and broadcaster in 1981. He worked for years with The Circus of Poets performance poetry group and Versewagon, the world's first mobile writing workshop, and then with Martyn Wiley as Yakety Yak. Since then he has worked in schools, theatres, arts centres, fields and front rooms. He is the presenter of BBC Radio 3's weekly poetry programme *The Verb* and has written comedy for radio and plays for the stage, and has worked extensively for BBC radio and television. He has collaborated widely with composers, artists and cartoonists. He is an honorary doctor of Sheffield Hallam University, Staffordshire University, York St John's University, Lancaster University, and Huddersfield University, and has been a Visiting Professor at Bolton University. Ian has been the poet-in-residence for English National Opera, The Academy of Urbanism, Humberside Police, and Barnsley FC. His many books of verse include *The Changing Problem* (Carcanet, 1980), *Dad, the Donkey's On Fire* (Carcanet, 1994), *Perfect Catch* (Carcanet, 2000), *Talking Myself Home* (John Murray, 2008), and *Jazz Peas* (smith|doorstop, 2014). He still lives in his hometown Barnsley.

T0164119

Also by Ian McMillan from Carcanet Press

Perfect Catch (2000)
I Found This Shirt (1998)
Dad the Donkey's on Fire (1994)
Selected Poems (1987)
Now it Can Be Told (1983)
The Changing Problem (1980)

IAN McMILLAN

*To Fold the Evening Star:
New & Selected Poems*

CARCANET

First published in Great Britain in 2016 by
Carcanet Press Limited
Alliance House, 30 Cross Street,
Manchester, M2 7AQ
www.carcanet.co.uk

This Lake Used to be Frozen: Lamps (2011), *Ah've Soiled Ma Breeks!* (2012)
and *Jazz Peas* (2014) were first published by smith|doorstop Books, and are
republished here with kind permission.

A CIP catalogue record for this book is available from the British Library.

ISBN 9781784101886

Typeset by XL Publishing Services, Exmouth
Printed and bound in England by SRP Ltd, Exeter

The publisher acknowledges financial assistance from Arts Council England

Contents

Dad, The Donkey's on Fire

(1994)

Kake Yourself Comfortable

Kome in. Sit Kown.
Kake yourself comfortable.

Kup of Kea? Bit of Kake?
Kilk? Kugar?

My problem? You Kish
to Kiscuss it?

Ah yes. The letter K.
Well, Kit all goes back

Ko Ky Khildhood. We were
very Koor. I only had one

Koy. A building Krick with
Ketters on. Except all the

Ketters had Keen Kubbed off,
except one. All my childhood

I Konly Kever saw Kone letter.
The letter S.

Why We Need Libraries

It is the mid-sixties, and it
does not matter which year exactly;

it may have been the year Mrs White
threw water on the cat. It may not.

At the bottom of the hill, opposite
the football factory which will close

in 1981 (although nobody knows this
because nobody can look into the future

in fact the future is a pair
of stout walking boots in a sealed box)

they are loading books from the old
library to take to the new library

which is near the new clinic and not
far from the new old folks' home

at the top of the hill. Yes, isn't
it symbolic that these new things are

at the top of the hill. Yes, isn't
that Ian McMillan and his pal Chris

Allatt waiting outside the empty new
library, the green tickets in their

fists, their eyes hungry for Biggles?
It is the mid-sixties, and the future

is waiting to walk away from us, briskly,
as though we smell funny, leaving the new

library to darken and crack into the old
library, closed on Saturday afternoons

Everyman I will go with thee and be thy
guide except on Saturday afternoons and

sometimes all day Mondays and sometimes
certain days for the need of money to pay

the people who open the doors to let the books
out. You never know what will happen, though,

because the future is a book in a private
library. Unless we can request that book

and borrow it and read it and read it.

Pit Closure as Art

In the centre of
the major retrospective
there is a door
which you open.

As you open it
certain nerves
in the face
are jangled
artificially:
you smile.

The smile becomes
the property of
The Artist.

Beyond the door
is a room
and another door.

You walk over to the door.

The catalogue says
'The door will not be locked'
but the catalogue also
is part of The Art.

The door is locked.
The door you came through
is locked. The Artist
has served The Art well.

As you stand there
certain nerves
in the eyes
are jangled
artificially:
you weep.

The tears become
the property of
The Artist.

You dig to keep warm.
The Artist arrests you for digging.
The Artist smashes your head
for pounding on the door.

The Artist prevents you
walking to the door.

All this is part of The Art.
The Artist has refined The Art well.

Lilian's Poem

A white box
with a bunch of violets on.
That's what I remember most.

The gaffer's name was Jones
and he wouldn't let you sing.
The girls liked to sing.

Nobody liked Mr Bowman.
He used to come and stand over you.
He stood over me.

A man came round every month
to put poison on the floor,
poison on the floor for the rats.

In the war men came to the door,
wanting their wives to come home,
wanting their wives to come home with them.

But I remember most
the violets
on the blue box.

(Lilian was a housebound woman I worked with when I was writer-in-residence
with Age Concern Leicester in 1987/8. The words are all hers.)

Death's Feet

I don't know. Sometimes you lie
and then you call it art. The man said
'Are you working on a novel?' and

I said, YES, O YES, YES I AM, YES.
And he said 'I hope it's one of your
Inspector McMillan novels. I just

love his jutting jaw, and the way
he solves it on the penultimate
page, leaving the last page free

for recipes.' And I said YES O YES
AYE AR THIS IS IT PAL AYE AR YES.
And he said 'Do you have a title

for it?' And I coughed and said
COUGH ER AR TITLE AR WELL THA
KNOWS SEMMAS COUGH ER death's feet.

Come stalky stalky
up the path
feeling your tie
in the moon's pale light.

Husband and Wife

We had to move, you see,
to be near the husband's work.
Literally, the husband's work
has taken him all over the place.

I am happy though enough.
I can sit at the window
and see blackbirds, clouds.
The husband's work, you see,

we have to move with it.
This time, we moved into the kitchen,
last time it was into the shed.

He calls his thoughts
'A letter from head office'.
The husband bends over his work
making it scream.

Tempest Avenue

It is 5 am, and I am standing
in the half-light bedroom
holding our son. He is finally asleep

and I lay him gently in the cot,
trying not to rattle the toy bear
attached to the bars. Next door

Mr Lowe is having a dream about
the glassworks at Stairfoot. Look:
all the workers have turned to glass,

what a strange dream. Across
the road, Mr Ford is cycling
out of his drive to the pit. He

cycles during the week, takes the car
at weekends. Down the street
my mam is standing at the kitchen

window, looking at our house, thinking
'Our Ian will be asleep. I hope
Mr Ford's squeaky cycle doesn't wake him

And I am being careful, so careful
with these words, laying them
gently into this poem, turning to the door.

Deaths from Ice Cream

Man killed by eating whole cone too
quickly. Woman died after slipping

on ice cream, falling under bus
carrying brass band. Child dies

sitting in snow trying to cool
dripping cone. Man killed by 99

hurled from hot air balloon by
lute player. Woman died after

argument with ice cream salesman
in Fife. Child dies of depression

after ice cream melts away. Man
killed by razor placed in ice cream

by crazed Methodist. Woman died
after eating three hundred ice creams

for a wager. Child dies after
falling into a giant vat of ice

cream during factory visit.

Ted Hughes is Elvis Presley

I didn't die
that hot August night.
I faked it,

stuffed a barrage balloon
into a jump suit.
Left it slumped
on the bathroom floor.

Hitched a ride on a rig
rolling to New York. Climbed
into the rig, the driver said
'Hey, you're…'
'Yeah, The Big Bopper. I faked it,
never died in that 'plane crash.
Keep it under your lid.'
I tapped his hat with my porky fingers.
He nodded. We shared a big secret.

Laid low a while in New York.
Saw my funeral on TV in a midtown bar.
A woman wept on the next stool but one.

'He was everything to me. Everything.
I have a hank of his hair in my bathroom
and one of his shoelaces
taped to my shoulderblade.'

'He was a slob,' I said.
She looked at me like I was poison.
'He was too, too big,' I said.
'He wanted to be small, like
a little fish you might find in a little pond.'

I needed a new identity.
People were looking at me.
A guy on the subway asked me
if I was Richie Valens.

So I jumped a tramp steamer
heading for England.
Worked my passage as a cook.
In storms the eggs
slid off the skillet.

Made my way to London.
Saw a guy, big guy, guy with a briefcase.
Followed him down the alley,
put my blade into his gut
and as the blood shot
I became him
like momma used to say
the loaf became Jesus.

I am Elvis Presley.
I am Ted Hughes.

At my poetry readings I sneer and rock my hips.
I stride the moors
in a white satin jump suit,
bloated as the full moon.

Bless my soul,
what's wrong with me?

At night I sit in my room
and I write, and the great bulbous me
slaps a huge shadow on the wall.

I am writing a poem
about the death of the Queen Mother
but it won't come right.

I look up. Outside a fox peers at me.
I sing softly to it,
strumming my guitar.

Soon, all the foxes
and the jaguars and the pigs
and the crows are gathering
outside my window, peering in.

I sing 'Wooden Heart', 'Blue Hawaii'.
There is the small applause
of paws and feathers.

I am Ted Hughes. I am Elvis Presley.
I am down at the end of a lonely street
and a jump suit rots in a southern coffin
as people pay their respects to a barrage balloon.

I sit here,
I can feel the evening shrinking me
smaller and smaller.
I have almost gone. Ted,
three inches long, perfect.
Elvis, Ted.

Visit

His moustache appears
to be hanging on nothing.

His heart appears to be
on a screen

like a film star
like Gene Kelly

in *Singing in the Rain*.
It appears to me

that Death almost
walked into this room

but if Death came
we would offer him

no orange juice. If
Death came we would

offer him no grapes.
It appears to me

that from this hospital window
you can see Barnsley

laid out like a stroke victim.
A stroke victim

dressed for a wedding
else a funeral.

Visiting time: you could
fry an egg on this clock,

it's so hot.
Yes, nurse, we're

going now. See you,
moustache. Get well

soon. The car park.
See, there is Death

stretching his stinking balaclava
tight over the town

like having a fat pig
sit on your face

like waking up
with the face of a dead pig

your moustache
hanging on nothing.

Early Train, Rain, Wombwell Station

'You could sell me the door.
I need the whole wall,
but I can make do with the door.'

The facts are in the title, you men.
As many facts as we need for now, thank you

very much. You men: regard me
with your feet, as those
are the parts of your bodies
which I am to kiss, and wash.

I am built, said the man
who was talking in the ranks,
to be whispered.
                 Like a secret!
I shout, pleased with my joke.

Are you not tired yet
of calling me 'you men'
she asked, holding me up
as though I was a hanged man.

By the neck, the train
glinted like an eye, and
the guard laughed, the
the driver laughed, the man with
the paper back laughed:

whispered like a secret!
whispered like, as he said,

a secret!

Poem Occasioned by the High Incidence of Suicide amongst the Unemployed

Now then, fatha, how's your Fred?
They found him in the kitchen
with a bullet in his head.

Now then, fatha, how's your John?
They found him in the river
with his donkey jacket on.

Now then, fatha, how's your Bill?
He jumped under a bus
on Spital Hill.

Now then, fatha, how's your Tom?
He blew hissen to pieces
with a homemade bomb.

Now then, fatha, how's your Pete?
He's hanging off a lamp post
on Market Street.

Now then, fatha, how's your Rex?
He strangled hissen
wi' his wedding kex.

Now then, fatha, how's your Stan?
He brayed hissen to death
wi' a watterin can.

Now then, fatha, wheers the wives?
They're cutting their sens
wi' carving knives.

Song for Roof Building (Collected in South Yorkshire Light Industry Park, Barnsley)

(To be accompanied by traditional hammering with roof-building tools)

Say a man has three shillings.
Would you tell me, would you tell me
who the man is with the three shillings?

Build part of the roof!

I know he is not me.
It is not me with the three shillings.
Not me with the three bob.

Build part of the roof!

I have seen them, the men
without three shillings
in this land with no poverty.

Build part of the roof!

I have seen them rubbing
their legs together
to keep warm, to make light.

Build part of the roof!

But this is only a song after all
to help me build this roof.
I do not care about the three shillings.

Build part of the roof!

Say a man has three shillings.
Would you tell me, would you tell me
who the man is with the three shillings?

Build part of the roof!

The Force of His Storm Knocked Me from My Stool

Please for this poem assume
that the word tired equals the word fat.

I went to see the doctor about feeling tired
all the time. Waking up tired. Falling
asleep holding a child's Barbie Horse.
Snoring through a guitar being painted.

The doctor advises me to squat on water.
'Feel it soak into your kex' he says. But
I don't wear kex I wear skirts and tops.
On fine days I wear skirts and tops and but and no hat.

Sometimes in a poem you have to put words in to make
t' rhythm. Sometimes you put in silly words to
make the rhyme. Like that word 'water'.

At home, the doctor moans he says he says
I feel so tired, so tired all the time.
His wife says Eat less you tired slobber.

For slobber read doctor, if you would.

At home, I squat in a wet dish.
The water soaks into my skirt. I'm still tired.

Hi, my name is Tony.
Did you know
that the inhabitants of my head
have fifty-two different words
for the word you know as 'tired'?

I hate it when Tony comes into a poem.
I have a capacity for hate.

Hi Tony. Come and sit here.
By the fire.

Moon River: Lives of the Great Comedians

Big Billy Death swigs a beer
of pint. Hey. Wordplay.
Get it?

Georgie Death eats a banana skin.
Visual humour. Get it?

Fanny Death does impressions.
Look! She's a chair! Look!
She's a table! Look!
She's gone! Get it?

Simon Death and the Death Boys.
Vocal harmony. Moon
River.
Get it?

Here come the memoirs
out of the traps like
(get it?) sauce from a bottle:

'I remember the time I played.
Now where was it. There in the middle
of the stage. A moon
suspended over a river. Audience had
no heads, just hats. Satire, I suppose.
Get it?'

'I remember the time. Stoke. Green
sky. Pottery, I suppose. Green sky,
though: green sky.

Pathos: geddit?'

'I recall a show in. Now where.
Waves lapped against something.
I am old and confused. I shall
leave you with a dance. Maestro.
Character humour. Get.'

Big Billy Death signs his face
on the bar. Georgie Death becomes
demented, eats the same banana
twice. Look! Fanny Death is
World War One.
Time for the song, boys, now.
Moon River, dying on its feet.

Henry's Skeleton, George's Leg

Every year they come
for the Head Teachers' conference:
Henry with his skeleton, George with his leg.

This used to be the big house, all the big windows
facing away from the pit, down the formal gardens.
Now they use it for courses, the Authority.
This year, George has put his leg
into a purple tracksuit bottom. Last year
it was a fishnet stocking. Every year
Henry sits the skeleton next to him at dinner.

It stares ahead as they discuss the National Curriculum.

I clear away the plates.
Last night
Henry took his skeleton out
and sat it on a bench in the grounds; an ambulance
screamed along the motorway. George's leg hung from a window.
I went home. I live in the village. My husband

wanted us to make love but I said No.
Not even if I wear my boots? he said.
No, I said, not even if you wear your boots.

My husband works in a sportswear factory.
Anything since the pit shut, he says.

Tonight I will wear a single fishnet stocking
and I will ask him to wear his purple tracksuit,
just the bottoms. He stole the tracksuit from work
under his coat with NCB on the back.

I can feel my bones under my skin.
My husband will not wear his tracksuit. In London
men in suits slam doors shut and put files
back in cabinets. Lights go out. Schools close.

George sleeps with his leg.
Henry hugs his skeleton close. So close.

My husband tugs on his boots and I look over the motorway
to where the pit used to be. I try to shield my breasts
from the noise of the boots.

My nipples will soon be very sore.

Jesus Died from Eating Curtains

My daughter said that
to me the other day.
As she said it my watch
stopped, and my wife
asked me what I was doing
a week on Sunday.

Synchronicity, I suppose
Jung would have called
it. My wife turned back
to the *Observer*, and
I wound my watch up.
For no reason at all

my daughter began to weep,
so I turned her cassette on
and I heard Postman Pat
say to Jess 'Jesus died
from eating curtains.' Okay
I didn't hear that. But

I am concerned about the
state of Poetry, hear?
I'm concerned about its
lack of ambition, about how
you don't often see the word
galoot or the word galosh

in poems. I'm concerned
about the shape of poems,
and I'm concerned that
poems often sound like
poems. Oh, galoot
galosh, galosh, galoot.

second stanza.' That's what he said,
leaning over me in the classroom,
puffing on his tweed pipe, the air

thick with twist and reek. 'Always
start your poems with the second
stanza, my boy, and you won't go far

wrong.' I pondered this in my rooms
in the University. I knew, just knew,
it was the Thirties. 'The Thirties

are a sort of second stanza, aren't
they?' I said to him. The air was
thick with twist and reek. 'I mean

if you take the War poets as a sort
of first stanza, maybe count the
Twenties as the bit of white space

you find between stanzas…' I was
developing a point, nicely. He looked
at me with eyes like carpet tiles.

'If Christ had only had a second
stanza,' he said, the air thick,
'he would only have risen again,

not died at all.' It was a famous
point. I remembered it all through
the war, the period of Austerity,

until the sixties, when my son
came home smoking Pot. I tried to
explain about the second stanza

but he said 'These are the Sixties,
daddy-o. These are today and now.
These days we leave out the

Point of Transit

fire door keep shut
fire door keep shut

It is a long way back
from the First World War
to here
standing with the young people
and their suitcases.

fire door keep shut

I converted all the cinemas
to sound, you know. All
the cinemas around here'.
Now it's all noise.
Skiing. That's
all downhill isn't it?
All downhill into something white?

fire door keep shut

In 1915 I looked up
and saw a young boy
struggling through the mud
with his suitcase.
Where are you going? I asked
but it was a silent film
and he answered in subtitles.

fire door keep shut

The words appeared in the mud by his trainers
I AM GOING SKIING
Skiing? That's all downhill isn't it?
All downhill into something white?

Downhill from the noise
of the trenches
downhill to the white
hair of an old man.

I carry my suitcase across his head.

I carry my suitcase across my head.
I walk across my head
to the fire door. It is shut.

I am on fire.
In subtitles the word FIRE
at my feet fifteen
times as I burn away.

Still Life Life

1

In front of a log fire
in Cumbria a Doctor
from New Zealand

has just said I went to
see a 3D movie once
but I sat in the front row

and I didn't see any of the film because
it all went on behind
my back.'

The word Ha
is issuing from the mouth
of a German girl

who is sitting next to
the Doctor from New Zealand.
It is followed by the word Ha.

2

I went to see a 3D movie once
but I sat in the front row
and I didn't see any of the film because
it all went on behind my back.

3

The log speaks:

I would rather burn in a fire
than hear this. I would rather
be fashioned into a bookend
than hear this. I would rather
be sawdust than hear this.

The Doctor speaks:

I went to see a 3D movie once
but I sat in the front row
and I didn't see any of the film because
it all went on behind my back.

Someone writes in a visitors' book:

I enjoyed myself very much. The food
was superb. The company was good. I have
not got enough space to tell you how much
I love staying here.

The shin of a dead man speaks:

Take these chains from my heart
and set me free.

The German girl speaks:

Ha Ha.

Realism (Nothing is Ever Finished)

Whoever said
Night is Black
wasn't kidding.

The children want
wallpaper. You buy them expensive toys
but all they want is wallpaper.

Black wallpaper. Night is really
an empty swimming pool
that you do not realise
is empty so you make
swimming motions in it.

Like this.
Like this.

But you are not wet.

Daddy, I want
a drink of wallpaper.

What kind do you want?
The kind with flowers on?
The kind that looks like a brick wall?

The kind we used to have in kitchens
with blazons of fruit? Bananas?

Any kind
Daddy.

Night is really
a box of spent matches.

No light, you see.

Daddy! More
wallpaper!

Dad, the Donkey's on Fire

There is a burning donkey
at the side of the canal.
It lights up the sky.

Look at the burning donkey.
In Donkey Language it is saying
'Look at me, you bastards,

I am on fire.'
Although it sounds like hee haw.

Stories

Poetry Matters

He pressed the briefcase and the catches sprang up with a loud click. Everyone on the bus looked at him. He fished out the handwritten instructions: 'Get on the 37 at the bus station. The school is two stops past the Red Lion.' He peered out of the window. It was foggy. He leaned forward and spoke to the man in front of him.

'Excuse me, are we anywhere near the Red Lion?'

The man didn't move his head. His cap was old and greasy. 'Are we, er... anywhere near the Red Lion, pal?'

'Don't talk to me about the bastard Red Lion! Just don't talk to me about the bastard Red Lion, okay?'

The man still hadn't moved. A woman across the aisle said 'Red Lion? It's here. I'm getting off here.'

As he walked past the man, the man said,

'Don't do it, pal. You may as well leave it in the bloody pot.' On the pavement the woman said,

'Was it Red Lion or Red Deer?'

'Red Lion.'

'Oh, I am sorry.'

He began to walk the long hill from the Red Deer to the distant school.

He felt the sweat making his hair prickle as he rang the bell. The window slid upwards.

'Can I help you?'

'Yes, er, my name's John Dixon. I'm the poet.'

'Yes?'

'er... I'm visiting the school today as... through the Writers-In-Schools scheme, to talk to the pupils.'

'You're a poet?'

John wondered if she always spoke in questions.

'I try to be.'

She didn't laugh. She turned to the girl who was typing.

'Do you know anything about a poet?'

The girl shook her head.

'Are you sure it's today?'

'The 21st, yes.'

'Yes. What teacher were you meeting?'

'Mr Harrison.'

'Mr Harrison? We don't have a Mr Harrison. We've got a Mrs Harrison. She takes maths. I don't think she'd have much use for a poet, do you?'

'You don't have a Mr Harrison.' It wasn't a question. A bell rang very loudly, drowning out most of her reply. He only caught the last three words.

'... Lord Arthur Morton?'

There was a pause as John Dixon tried to work out a reply. He thought it must be a literary question.

'I'm afraid I'm not familiar with his work.' She didn't smile.

'I said, do you want to be at Lord Arthur Morton? Are you quite sure you want to be at Lord Arthur Morton?'

'I'm sorry, I don't...'

'This is Lord Arthur Morton School. The old grammar. Is it Brookvale you're wanting?'

He seized on the familiar word.

'Brookvale, yes!'

'Just across the road. I should have guessed it would have been Brookvale. They have poets and that kind of thing. I wouldn't have thought they'd have been having one today, though. They once had an arts festival, I believe.'

She pronounced Arts Festival as though it was a crippling disease.

John turned and ran.

A tall man was standing at the school entrance looking worried. John dashed up to him.

'Mr Harrison? John Dixon. Sorry I'm late; my son's been ill.'

He couldn't admit that he'd been to the wrong school. Harrison shook John's hand and began to hurry him down the corridor. Mr Harrison spoke very quickly.

'Did you get the letter? We've had to make a few changes to the schedule.'

'I didn't get a letter.'

'What? Didn't you?' He stopped walking. He looked as though he was going to weep. He thumped the wall.

'Oh, the bloody secretary. The bloody, bloody secretary!'

'It doesn't matter. It'll be okay.' They began to walk again, faster.

'Anyway, if you didn't get the letter, I don't suppose it matters. Nothing bloody matters!' He laughed, extremely loudly.

'So what am I doing first?'

'First you're reading to the first year, then you'll be doing a workshop with the second year, then after lunch it's two workshops with the third year.'

This time it was John's turn to stop. He had gone cold.

'First years? I don't usually work with first years.'

'Oh, you'll be okay. Thick as planks the lot of them. They really are a dumb bloody year.'

'I suppose…'

'They don't know anything about you. There hasn't been time. They're sitting in a drama studio so I suppose the thick sods think they're getting a play.'

'Can you introduce me?'

'Can't you just get on with it?'

'It's nice to be introduced. It gets it off to a good start.'

'Okay then, if you like.' They approached a door. From behind it John could hear the sound of slow, rhythmic handclapping. They walked into the room. There was a quick, empty silence, and then the room exploded into laughter. Someone shouted 'I fancy him!' and someone else said 'He looks a right wally!' John scuttled to the corner of the room like an insect. He looked at the rows of children. They looked huge. They looked to be in their early thirties. First years. What the hell do you say to first years? He was used to working with sixth formers; polite and shy or volatile and dismissive but always in some kind of relationship to his status as a famous poet. Harrison was yelling at the rows of laughing faces.

'Right. I'm waiting. Thank you. Thank you.' The noise gradually subsided. The room became terribly quiet. John opened his briefcase and the catches sprang up with a loud crack. Mr Harrison spoke, too loudly for the echoing room:

'Right. We've got this poet on now. He's turned up. Poets are supposed to be late, anyway. I don't know much about him. Here he is.'

John walked across the floor to the table in the complete angry silence. Someone whispered, loud enough for him to hear, 'He looks a boring bastard.' He opened his mouth, cleared his throat.

'Thank you Mr Harrison, er…'

The laughter bellowed at him again.

John and the man who wasn't Mr Harrison walked into the staffroom. People began to speak to each other in indecipherable code.

'Got the eighteens?' said a very old man in a track suit. The man who wasn't Mr Harrison nodded.

'They're over in K7. I brought the Hunstanton, too.'

John stood on his own.

'Sorry I thought you were Mr Harrison,' he said to the smoky air near the man's back.

'He thought I was Harrison!'

'Christ!' the man in the tracksuit laughed.

'What is your name?' asked John.

'er… Frank Smith.'

'Bloody Hell!' The man in the tracksuit seemed shocked. Frank Smith said, 'I'm not sure who you're with next. Sorry that last lot weren't too keen. Ignorant little sods. Mind you, I think you were a bit over their heads. Sorry they got a bit restless.'

'I thought they might have asked a few more questions.'

'Yes. Would you like a cup of coffee?'

'Yes please. Black. No sugar.'

'Sorry, they only do white. Out of a big bloody teapot. Look, would you look after yourself for a bit. I've got to see somebody. Harry could…' He looked around but the man in the tracksuit had gone.

'Anyway, you'll be okay. After break, either me or somebody else will be down to get you for the workshop. Actually it probably won't be me, but somebody'll come…' he backed out of the door as he spoke. The bell rang. Everyone in the staffroom moaned. A man turned to John and said,

'Always the same, you just get to the bloody coffee…'

'I've got Darren Southwell next,' said a small dark-haired woman, 'pray for me.'

They all laughed. John laughed. The first man spoke again. 'Darren Southwell? No, you're okay. Moira's put him down for that creative writing workshop. Some poor poet coming along to try and drill some culture into us. Poor bugger.'

'Bloody hell! Darren'll eat him alive!'

'Mind you, have you heard how much he's getting? Forty quid!'

'Hey, we're in the wrong game here! What's that line again… I wandered lonely as a… what?'

'Pillock?'

They all laughed. John didn't laugh. He'd asked for £50. The dark haired woman spoke again.

'I wouldn't have thought they'd have had a poet today, what with…'

'Oh, sod that!'

'So to speak!' They all laughed again. The woman turned to John. 'Are you here for the interview?'

'Yes,' John lied.

'Don't come and work in this place, it's a madhouse.'

'And a dump.'

'Mind you, there'll be a few more vacancies soon; we're all going to be poets.' They laughed again, then moved quickly out of the room. The staffroom was now empty except for a woman collecting coffee cups, three young men in suits, and John. The men in suits were obvious interviewees.

John glanced at his watch. 11:05. The lesson ended at five past twelve. With a bit of luck he wouldn't have to do too much. He sat down and began to leaf through the *Times Educational Supplement*.

At 11:15 he began to worry, began to feel guilty. For £50, even for £40, he ought to be working. One of the interviewees leaned over and said 'You should have worn a suit, you know, mate. They don't go much on casual dress here. Some places you could get away with it, but not at this place.'

John was trying to think of a reply when a tall, nervous man ran in. He began to shout in a theatrical voice.

'Why isn't that stupid man with 2C? The wretched poet! He seems to have sloped off somewhere…'

Sloped off. Wretched. John noted the anachronisms,
'I'm the poet,' he said. 'I was told to wait here and somebody would fetch me.'
'Who told you that? That's not what I said! Who told you?'
'Frank Smith.'
The tall man swayed as though he had been hit. He put his hand to his mouth in a swift gesture, then turned and ran from the room. John didn't know what to do, what he had said to offend the man. He stood for a second and then walked out after him. He had the impression that the man had gone right. He turned right and walked briskly down the corridor. He glanced at his watch. 11:23. He'd soon have no time left to write any poetry with them. He realised he didn't really know what he was looking for. He turned to a boy who had suddenly appeared beside him.
'Excuse me. Do you know where I might find the second year?'
'Which second year?'
'How do you mean?'
'I mean what form does it reckon to be?'
'I'm not sure.'
'I should try the office. If there's anybody there. They're probably all at the funeral.'
'Another poet?'
'What?'
'It doesn't matter. Thanks. Where *is* the office, by the way?'
'Down there, on the left.'
John walked into the office. The tall man was sitting at a desk. He was clutching a cup of coffee. His eyes were red. He looked up at John.
'Are you satisfied?'
'I'm sorry; I don't know what you mean. I'm looking for that second year.'
'Oh, sod the bloody second year!'
A woman came in.
'You shouldn't upset yourself, Mr Harrison. Look, I think it would be best if you went home.'
'I don't want to go home. I want to carry on as if nothing. Had. Happened.' He spoke the last three words very slowly.
'Perhaps you ought to have gone to the funeral… you really should have…'

'No. It had to end there. With him.'

John felt like an intruder.

'Is it Frank Smith who's dead? And are you Mr Harrison?'

The telephone rang. Nobody answered it. The tall man smiled.

'I should be more hospitable, Mr Dixon. I'm normally here to welcome my poets…'

He put both hands to his face. He began to sob. He rubbed his eyes savagely.

'I think it's best if you go now, Mr Dixon. Really, I do,' the woman said.

'No. No. He should stay,' said Mr Harrison.

'I think it is best if you go,' said the woman.

The Route to Work

They were discussing it again when he got in the car. Paul jerked the car away from the kerb, almost, David thought, as though he was jerking a dog away from something interesting in a patch of grass.

'She's a very stubborn girl,' said Paul, glancing at the rearview mirror. David closed his eyes and thought about the day ahead. John smiled and tried, really tried, to make a joke. Paul ignored it.

'Our final authority has to be Jesus Christ in matters like this,' he said. He said *Jesus Christ* in an undertone, like he was swearing. 'But if you look at the reason St Paul says it…' said John.

'The reason St Paul says it,' said Paul as though he was about to bellow. He didn't bellow. He went quiet. He spoke again, quietly.

'The reason is that the women in the early church…' John interrupted him.

'Yes, in the early church they were so excited about their new-found freedom in Christ. They jumped around and made a lot of noise, and that's why St Paul says they should wait until later to ask. Ask questions at home.'

Outside, an old postman struggled with a bulging sack.

They drove up the hill past Wombwell station. The sky was a slab of red in the earlyish morning light. John tried again to make a joke but Paul was determined to keep the mood serious.

'I ought to tell my wife about that obey bit,' said David. He felt suddenly uncomfortable. He put his hand in his jacket pocket and pulled out a tomato. He felt embarrassed. He also felt a little sad. He opened his carrier bag and dropped the tomato in.

'In 1662 women were chattels,' said Paul, his face reddening. I tell you this, it was all I could do to keep my temper...'

It seemed to David that Paul was saying things in the wrong order, out of sequence. He wasn't making a lot of sense.

'They did everything the man asked them to. When they married the man took all their goods as though they were his own.' They slowed down at the traffic lights on Platts Common. On the left a fat man in a vivid red track suit pounded along the pavement. On the right a woman carried a box of vegetables into a shop from a van.

'Things have changed today...' The lights changed. They moved. Paul continued to speak. The words seemed clearer now.

'He ought to understand the relationship between a man and a woman, that the relationship has changed...'

David felt in his pocket again. Another tomato, big and ripe. Not a good salad one but okay for frying. He dropped it in the carrier bag. There was a pause. John spoke.

'So, what's the next step going to be?'

David thought about the journey to work and the idea of the Journey to Work. The idea of the sacredness, holiness of the Journey. It seemed silly to point out to himself that if you worked in the same place for a long time you never varied your route to work. Or the mode of transport. Instead of car every day, this route every day, it could be car one day, bike the next, some days roller skates. Some days a giant airship disfiguring the sky over Grenoside.

'Well, they're coming down this weekend. They're going to see him.' Paul appeared to be changing more gears than there were in the car. The car had slowed to a halt in traffic and David was able to look into the house on his left. There were four tomatoes ripening on the windowsill. An old man slumped in an armchair, asleep in front of breakfast television.

'But I tell you this, she can be a very stubborn girl.'

Two more tomatoes, one in each pocket. One seemed to be

striped, but it couldn't be. No, it wasn't. He checked again. Yes, it was.

Yes, it was.

'They don't understand the changing relationship between men and women.'

They slowed down. Debbie was waiting. She climbed into the car. It was the first time they had seen each other for three days. They all said Hello. It was like a poem consisting of only the word Hello and no other words, or a list containing only the word Hello.

'I hated the whole thing. I'm absolutely knackered,' said Debbie.

'That's a shame. You were looking forward,' said John.

'The weather must have been appalling,' said Paul.

'The hailstones were hurting our faces, one bit…'

'We're still in the middle of the Obey Debate here,' said John.

'She shouldn't bother with it at all…'

The sky was getting redder. Do I understand that? Do you understand any of this? Do I understand that at this point, or around this point, the story changes? It changes.

We are in the mind of the man in the house. The old man, slumped, asleep. The television is watching him. David is talking to the man and it is as though he is interviewing him. The man is speaking in his head. David is speaking in his head.

'I remember before the war when all this was tomatoes. Before even this road had been thought of, before the man who painted the white lines on the road had even been born. Tomatoes, all of it. And then the planners came. And they decided to knock down all those lovely rows of terraced tomatoes and throw up those high rise tomatoes in their place. And the tomato always breaks down. You have to climb the tomatoes. And that's no good if you're my age.'

'What do you remember about the war?'

'In a crater, up to my waist in mud. Tomatoes bursting overhead. My mate lying beside me, dead as a tomato. Then a bullet got me, right in the chest. And I thought "I'm a goner. My tomato's up." But there wasn't any blood. I felt in my pocket and do you know what? My grandfather's old tomato had saved me. The bullet was lodged in it. That tomato he brought in 1867 from Wales, and gave me on my fourteenth birthday when he was too old to hold a fork. It was a miracle.'

'What can you tell me about love?'

'Not much. This. My old wife. When she was my young wife, standing there naked and superb on our wedding night. She held a tomato in her hand and I sat on a stool drawing her on clean white paper. So as not to forget it. Her there, naked and superb, and me concentrating on the tomato, drawing it with great care. What you might call infinite care.'

'And what can you tell me about Death?'

'My old mum used to say "Open any cupboard and you'll find it" and she meant Death. When Len died who should be the one to break down at the grave but Betty. "I loved him more than I loved my…'

'Tomatoes?'

'No.'

You must agree that to go back to the car now would be a betrayal. To return to that debate on whether Paul's daughter should agree to obey her husband would be a slap in the face for this story. We cannot stay with the old man either. He has discarded the tomato motif. The emblem that I've been trying to carve into the story like a mark in a piece of silver has gone. We can go nowhere. To end, though, to tie the story up, I will walk over to Len's funeral in the pouring rain.

It was raining. The kind of rain that loves funerals. I broke through the hedge and began to walk briskly towards the little gang of people at the graveside. I was in my shirtsleeves and I was soaked. They were just lowering the coffin in. Betty was crying. A strong man had his arm around her shoulders. Betty began to speak.

'I loved him. I loved him more than I loved my…'

It is right that her words are lost in a crash of sobbing from the strong man. I lean over towards Betty's mouth, placing my ear against it like you would place a limpet shell over the mouth of a plastic bottle. I hear nothing. She loved him. Perhaps that is enough.

Whatever Happened to Freddie Galloway?

It was 1962, and I was in Mrs Hudson's class at Low Valley Juniors; it was Monday morning, it was raining and it was the day the school photographer came. My mam stood there with the rainmate in her hand, and I stood there sobbing.

'I'll look daft in a rainmate,' I said, my breath coming in great heaving gulps; 'I'll look like a lass.' My mam wasn't impressed.

'You'll not look like a lass! How can you look like a lass with knees like that?' She arranged my hair one last time and then placed the rainmate carefully over it.

'You are not going to look like Alfalfa for your school photo; you are not going to sit on Auntie Mabel's mantelpiece like a scarecrow!' All the relatives got my school photo for an additional Christmas present; me smiling out on front rooms from the Borders of Scotland to the North Derbyshire coalfield. I had the kind of hair that stuck up like a brush, so on the weekend before the photos I always had to go to Mad Geoff's for my hair cut. I never fathomed why they called him Mad Geoff, except that he always wore a dicky bow which I suppose sets you apart in a village like ours.

I'd gone after school on the Friday night; Mad Geoff was empty except for Bing, sitting there in his trilby and serenading us with 'Three Coins in The Fountain'. When we came in Bing stopped singing and, looking at my mother, said to Geoff, 'Has tha gow owt for't weekend?' and Geoff said, 'Aye, a country cottage.' My mam stared into space.

When I got into the chair Geoff said, 'What does tha want then, Richard? Tony Curtis? Dickie Valentine? Fabian? Elvis?' I was about to say Fabian when my mother said 'He wants a light trim. A very light trim.' Bing repeated the order: 'He wants a light trim, Mad. An extremely light trim.' Geoff was famous for his enthusiastic cutting, and anything other than a light trim came out like what my dad called a barrack room special.

As Geoff trimmed and his clippers buzzed I heard Bing telling my mam about The Daz Man.

'They reckon they'll be coming round this area next week, Mrs M., so you'd better keep your eye open for 'em.'

'They'll not be coming round here,' said my mam scornfully. 'The rent man's the only one that comes round here.'

'Well, you'd better have your packet of Daz ready, Missus,' Bing piped up, 'if you complete that slogan they'll give you a ten bob note.'

Geoff just missed my ear with his clippers. 'Aye, and if you believe that you'll stand for't' egg under't' cap,' and then whipped the sheet off me and said, 'Does that want any jollop on it?' I was about to say yes when my mam said, 'He does not! It took two days to wash it out last time!'

'Who's the Daz Men, mam?' I asked as we walked home through the park.

'It's just some daft stuff off the telly. Some soft articles who come knocking on your door because they've got nowt better to do.'

Now it was Monday morning and I was walking to school in the rain with a rainmate on. I tried to hide behind my mam as we caught up with Robert Doughty. If he saw me in a rainmate he'd never let me forget it. As we drew level with Mrs Doughty and Robert my mam turned to me in triumph.

'There, Richard. I told you it was a good idea.'

There was Robert Doughty, the cock of class six, with a rainmate on. A pink rainmate. He looked at me with murder in his eyes.

In the cloakroom my mam took the rainmate off and folded it up. She patted my hair nervously.

'What time's the photographer coming, anyway?' she asked.

'Two o'clock, Mrs Matthewman,' said Robert, still with his rainmate on. He looked like a sea anemone.

'Two o'clock?' said my mam in horror. 'How are you going to keep your hair tidy till two o'clock?'

'I'll make sure Richard keeps his rainmate on,' said Robert, angelically.

Assembly was taken by Miss Parkin. We sang 'When a Knight won his Spurs', said some prayers and then Miss Parkin looked at us and said, 'Well, I can see you've all remembered that the school photographer is coming today. And this year we're going to try something a little bit different. As well as the individual photos, we're going to do some class photographs. That means in years to come, when you're all big boys and girls, you'll be able to look at the pictures with fond memories. Now, who knows what fond memories are?' A forest of hands shot up, mainly from the youngest infants. Miss Parkin pointed to Mary Till, who was straining her arm upwards and snapping her fingers enthusiastically.

'Yes, Mary. What are Fond Memories?'

Mary looked doubtful.

'Fond Memories, Mary. Do you know what we mean when we say Fond Memories?'

'Seven,' said Mary.

'That's nearly right Mary. Have another go. Fond Memories.'

'Seventy ten,' said Mary, triumphantly. Miss Parkin signalled to Mrs Hinchcliffe to begin the music, and we filed out to Ravel's *Bolero*.

Everybody was excited about the photographer coming; we'd all come in our best clothes, and at least five lads in our class had been brought to school with rainmates on. Mrs Hudson said that we all looked a picture already and Noel Ramsden said we looked like Fond Memories and Mrs Hudson smiled and gave him a star.

At playtime Mrs Hudson warned us: no running about, no fighting, no donkey rides, no football. Robert Doughty came up.

'Where's your rainmate, Richard? I promised your mam you'd wear it.'

I tried to ignore him. The rainmate was in my pocket. Robert walked right up to me, pressing himself against me.

'I said where's your rainmate. You've got to wear your rainmate or your dad'll get his belt out. I heard your mam tell my mam. Get your rainmate on.'

I felt the tears welling up in my eyes.

'It's not raining,' I said, quietly.

'Put it on anyway, or I'll squeeze your balloons.'

I didn't know what that meant but it sounded painful. I got the rainmate out and put it on. Everybody laughed. The tears splashed down my cheeks. Mrs Robinson came out and rang the bell, and we all lined up. Everybody was looking at me. Mrs Robinson said, ' You can take your rainmate off now Richard, but that's a very sensible boy for putting it on.'

I wiped my eyes with my cuff and allowed myself a little smile.

We'd just started back after play when a big boy came round with a note. Mrs Hudson read it and said, 'Will you all please stop what you're doing, please. Now.' We all sat quietly and looked at Mrs Hudson. She had bright red lips which were famous throughout the school. In those days most teachers didn't wear lipstick and if they did it was something pale and subtle. Not Mrs Hudson: she lit the classroom up like a beacon as she welcomed us each morning. And now those bright red lips were pursed like she didn't understand the message that the big boy had brought.

'This note has just come round from Miss Parkin, and it's very serious so I want you all to pay attention.' She read it carefully. 'There are some people in the village with a doz hats but you are on no account to take one of them if offered.' Mrs Hudson put the note down and looked at us. 'Doz. That's a dozen.'

She looked at me.

'How many hats is a dozen, Richard?'

'Daz hats,' I said. I felt like Mary Till.

'Yes, all right. How many is a doz.'

'They Daz hats, Mrs Hudson,' said Freddie Galloway.

'I know there's a doz, Freddie, but how *many* is that?' I could see that Mrs Hudson was getting exasperated. She'd moved from the Forest of Dean when her husband's pit shut and sometimes she couldn't understand a word we said.

'It's Daz like off the telly, Miss,' said Freddie. 'Blokes are coming round and if you get words reight they gi thi a big hat. It's only for a laugh.'

Mrs Hudson looked more puzzled than ever. She folded the note up and put it on her desk.

'Anyway, Class Six; these people need their hats. You are not to take one. Now get on with your poems about "My Favourite Feeling".'

Dinnertime came round quickly. I gobbled my dinner down and went out to play; the weather was still dismal, and the supply teacher from Huddersfield was bundled up in scarves and a big fawn duffel coat. We called him Green Un because he looked just like the man from the Sue Ryder Home who sold the Green Un outside Harry and Jud's shop on a Saturday afternoon. I wandered up to the gate, and looked out. The pit bus went past taking the afternoon shift, and I waved to my dad. He didn't wave back, just sat there staring into space.

Behind the pit bus there was a brightly coloured van that looked just like a packet of soap powder, driven by a man in a white trilby. It was the Daz Hats! The van stopped outside the gates and the man got out. Word spread instantly and loads of us crowded round the gate.

'Who'd like a hat? Anybody like a hat?'

We were hesitant at first, then Noel Ramsden said, I'll have one!' The man put his hand into a bag and pulled out a big blue hat with WASHES WHITER on it. Noel put it on and we all laughed. Noel said, 'I don't know the slogan' and the man said, 'It doesn't matter, kid. It doesn't matter. Let's just get rid of some of these bloody hats!'

We all recoiled a bit at the rude word, but then surged forward when he started to pull the hats out of the bag. I got one: it was too big and it flopped over my ears but it didn't seem to matter. We were all running about and laughing. Bill Lillee had two hats on, and Robert Doughty was throwing his up in the air and catching it.

Suddenly we all went quiet. Miss Parkin was standing there, her face pale with fury.

'Just what do you think you are doing Keith Barlow?' she said to the man with the hats. He looked sheepish.

'Just giving out these hats like for a joke Miss Parkin.'

'You've been in the George by the state of you, as well. You've not changed since I used to teach you, Keith Barlow, you've not changed a bit. Now get away and take those silly hats with you.'

He climbed into the van and drove off. We were very impressed by the fact that Miss Parkin seemed to know everybody in the world. She turned her anger on us: 'I'm surprised at you, I really am. Now give me those ridiculous hats and you can go back to your classrooms because the photographer will be here in a minute. Fond memories, children, remember? Fond memories.'

I passed her my hat but I was surprised to see that some people were taking a huge risk by stuffing theirs into their pockets or down their jumpers. One fell on the floor and Miss Parkin picked it up with a smile. We filed into the classroom.

Mrs Hudson licked her finger and smoothed my hair down as we queued up to go to the photographer. She smiled at me, and I smiled back. The photographer had a little horse puppet and he shouted, 'Watch the Horsey!' to make us look happy on the picture. After all the individual ones were done, we had to group together for the class photo. The little ones sat at the front, and I stood at the back with the other big lads. I had Robert Doughty on one side, and Freddie Galloway on the other.

Once the photographer had us all settled he waggled the horse puppet and shouted, 'Watch the Horsey!' and at that moment lots of things happened at once.

Freddie Galloway pulled a Daz hat out of his pocket and put it on and at the same time Robert Doughty fished one out of his cardigan and jammed it on my head. Miss Parkin ran across the room like she was being chased and the camera flashed. I'll always remember that moment, and what it led to: Robert and Freddie being sent home, and the start of Freddie's long decline that ended in 1991 when the pit shut and he took to wandering between the George, the Sportsman and the Drop through the long afternoons.

When Miss Parkin died, her sister came to see me. I'd just started teaching and I was doing some work at the kitchen table. She came in and said, 'Miss Parkin wanted you to have this; she always knew you'd amount to something.'

It was the picture. Me with the hat crushed on my head, Robert Doughty looking wicked, and Freddie Galloway smiling innocently beneath his big blue brim. Washes Whiter. Fond Memories.

Grisp the Wheel at Ten Past Two

The car horn hooted outside. I didn't move. I stood looking at myself in the mirror. The spot on my neck was huge. Vesuvius, the kids at school called it. I'd been teaching there two terms. The longest two terms of my life. September 1977 to April 1978. At least thirty years to go. Then, sitting on the bus on the way home the other night, a gang of big women from the tennis-ball factory got on. They always got on at that time. They smelled of rubber and scent, and they took over the bus. One sat next to me. She stared at my neck. I felt myself getting red. The woman in front was showing the woman next to her photos of the Queen Mother's recent visit to Barnsley. 'That's her hand, waving,' she was saying. 'Eee, hasn't she got lovely gloves on!' I tried to lean over to see the pictures and the woman next to me said, 'What's that on your neck?'

The two women in front turned round slowly. My neck was more interesting than the Queen Mother's gloves, waving. I stood up and got off the bus, a mile before the house.

The horn hooted again. I went outside. The driving instructor's car was white, and not as new as it could have been. 'Don's Driving School,' it said on top. Don himself sat inside; he was a small, balding man, and I noticed that he was wearing the biggest pair of sandals I'd ever seen. He looked at me, then looked at my neck, and sucked in his breath.

'I don't get many your age,' he said. 'It's mainly kids, just past their seventeenth birthday. It's mainly kids.'

All my mates in the lower sixth had got driving lessons for their seventeenth birthday. Dave Sunderland had got a car. It sat in the drive as he took lesson after lesson and failed test after test. He washed it every Sunday and always sent for AA road maps for his holiday with his mam, and then sat studying them on the coach as the car gathered rust and a cat had kittens underneath it. Eventually he passed and drove to the shop in triumph for his mother's regular order of Advocaat. And that left only me. I once asked a girl out in that summer after I left school and before I went to college. I said I'd meet her at the bus stop opposite the cemetery. She looked at me with withering contempt and said 'You can't be a man with a ticket in your hand.' Her parents got the *Manchester Guardian* and she was going to Art College in Falmouth.

Don shifted his sandals and looked at me again and said, 'Not many your age like I say, not many your age.'

'Well, I'm fed up of the bus,' I said. 'Slow, overcrowded, and I've to wait in the bus station for another one. Two buses to catch, an hour and forty minutes door-to-door and it's only eight miles.'

'I bet kids on the bus take the michael out of that thing on your neck and all,' he said. 'I bet kids on the bus take the michael.' He drove us to a layby just outside the village. We changed places. As I got out I noticed that his sandals flapped like flippers.

'Right. Comfortable?'

'Er… yes.'

'OK. This is the brake. This is the clutch. This is the accelerator.'

My neck was killing me; a heavy, continual pain that made it hard to grasp what he was saying.

'I said, turn it on. Use the key. Turn it on using the key.'

I almost said, no, I've changed my mind, got out and walked

away. I didn't really want to learn to drive. I enjoyed being in cars, enjoyed being a passenger, but being a driver, in charge of a lethal machine that could kill and maim, no thanks. But I thought about the bus station in February and the factory women and the bloke with the stick who always saw me on the bus and made a point of sitting next to me and showing me the scars on his back, and I turned the engine on and tried to proceed into the traffic, as I'd seen my dad do many many times.

The car leaped forward like a kangaroo and there was a terrible crashing of gears. Don grabbed the wheel from me and a huge artic-ulated lorry went past, blaring its horn.

Don was white and sweating. I thought driving instructors were meant to be calm.

'Bloody Hell Fire, I mean Bloody Hell Fire! What were you trying to do? Kill us both? We'd have ended up looking like that thing on your neck if that artic had flattened us. We'd have looked like that thing on your neck if that artic had flattened us. That thing on your neck.' I noticed that when Don got agitated he repeated things even more.

Somehow we got into the stream of traffic and crawled down the road. Don was a bit calmer, although a twitch had started ticking away under his left eye. I hunched over the wheel like a cop in Highway Patrol.

'Relax,' said Don. 'Relax. Relax.' I tried to relax.

'You're not holding the wheel properly. You're not holding it properly. You've got to grisp the wheel at ten past two.'

'Don't you mean grip the wheel at ten to two?'

Don's twitch went into top gear. 'Grisp it, grisp it. Grisp the wheel at ten past two. Grisp the wheel at ten past two!' I grisped it, both hands round the right side of the wheel, and he slapped my hand.

'Like this, like this!' he said, holding his hands up in the ten-to-two position. We drove on. I stalled at traffic lights, drove in first gear. I felt my collar chafing at my neck. The hour was almost over. 'Turn left up this hill,' said Don. 'Turn left up this hill. Turn left up this hill.' I turned left. Snape Hill, very steep indeed. The car juddered and began to lose power. 'Change gear. Change gear. Change gear. Change gear,' said Don, his twitch dancing madly under his eye. I was in second gear and the hill was too steep. I needed to get into first. I changed gear. Into fourth. The gearbox almost exploded and the gearstick leaped out of my hand. The car stopped. A bread van almost crashed into us, and then swerved by, the driver gesturing madly. Don gestured back, theatrically, giving a deliberate two finger salute with the fingers spread very wide and the hand going up and down very slowly. It made me think of the Queen Mother's gloved hand and I had to stifle a giggle. I coughed.

'It's not funny. It's not funny. This car is my living. My living.'

'I'm sorry.'

'Well be more careful. Be more bloody careful.'

We got slowly to the top of the hill. Don wiped his face with a big hanky. 'Slow down here. Pull in here.'

'What for?'

'Just slow down here. Pull in here. Pull in here.'

The car ground to a halt outside the Methodist chapel. On the notice board there was a poster which read 'Well Done is Better Than Well Said'.

'I won't be a minute,' said Don, clambering out of the car, sandals flapping. I wound the window down and leaned out.

'Why, where are you going?'

'I've got to get some sticks,' he said. At least that's what I think he said. He went round the back of the chapel. I sat there in the pale sun and felt the thing on my neck. It hurt. It was sort of soft round the bottom and then hard round the top. Like a nipple.

After a while I noticed a woman looking at me through the open window. It was the woman who'd sat next to me on the bus.

'You want to see a doctor with that,' she said. I tried to look away, as though I'd got something phenomenally interesting in the glove box. Her eyes bored into my neck. 'My uncle had one of them. The doctor had to clean it out with a wire.'

I couldn't stand it anymore. Where the hell was Don? I got out of the car. Where was Don going to get sticks in a chapel?

The side door of the chapel was open, so I went in. The room felt cool and smelt of polish. I could hear a voice muttering at the far end of the big room. It was Don. He was standing in the pulpit reading something, but you could hardly hear him. I walked down the aisle towards him. An old lady in a big blue hat looked at me and smiled. I noticed that someone was lying in one of the pews, asleep.

It was Phil Allsop, the Methodist Sunday School leader. As I looked at him, he woke up. I went to school with Phil; he was always a bit holy. He once told Mr Drinkwater that he should take Jesus into his life and Mr Drinkwater clipped him round the head with a hardback copy of *The White Company* by Sir Arthur Conan Doyle. Phil sat up, rubbing his eyes. He looked exhausted. He worked in the offices at the bed factory because his mother used to say he was delicate. I noticed that he deliberately wasn't looking at the thing on my neck.

'All right, Richard. It's good to see you in the house of the Lord. What brings you here?'

'I'm looking for Don. I'm supposed to be having a driving lesson with him.' Phil looked distressed.

'Well, that's just not fair. He told me he'd cleared his diary. We're only up to Numbers as well.'

I was baffled. 'I'm sorry, but I don't know what you're talking about.'

'I did the whole night shift. Bill Ellis was supposed to do the four a.m. section but glory knows where he got to… I had to do all night on my own and now I don't know if I'm coming or going. And Don was meant to do three hours this morning and he was almost an hour late. It's just not on!' He sounded close to tears.

'I still don't know what you're on about,' I said.

Phil looked at me as though he was seeing me for the first time. His eyes were almost shutting as he spoke.

'I'm sorry. I'm so tied up in this thing. It's to raise funds for the Sunday School outing. We're having a sponsored neck reading.'

'Pardon?'

'A sponsored bible reading. The whole lot from Genesis to Revelation; should take about four days altogether. We're supposed to do two hour shifts but I've been quite badly let down by my volunteers.'

'You said sponsored neck reading.'

Further down the church in the pulpit Don stopped muttering and shouted, 'I won't be a minute. I'll just get to the end of this chapter. I'll just get to the end of this chapter.' Phil turned to him in despair.

'Oh, Don! Can't you stay another hour? I've got Violet Mullis coming at twelve. Her sister's bringing her from the home.'

'I can't. I can't. I've got to get Stirling Moss here home and then I've got another lesson with him that won the pools. I've got to get Stirling Moss here home and then I've got another lesson with him that won the pools.' He put his head down and carried on muttering, turning a page. Phil sat down heavily; he looked older, somehow. In fact he looked the spitting image of photographs I'd seen of his Grandad Allsop in the trenches. It must have been the quality of light in the chapel. I know one thing: my neck was giving me some hell.

'Don't worry about it, Phil,' I said. 'I'll get the bus home. I don't think me and driving are meant for each other.' I felt in my pocket and gave him some change. More than I intended, actually. 'Here, have this for the Sunday School outing.'

He smiled, and the years seemed to fall away from him. He looked at the money and I remembered that after Mr Drinkwater had hit him with the copy of *The White Company* Phil had smiled and said, 'I forgive you, Mr Drinkwater, you didn't know what you were doing.' So Mr Drinkwater hit him again with Lamb's *Tales from Shakespeare*. Maybe he'd end up a saint. Phil, not Mr Drinkwater.

Phil looked at the money. 'Well, every bit helps,' he said, 'but we've a long way to go before we reach our neck.'

I went outside before I hit him. I knew how Mr Drinkwater felt. The sun had gone in and it was blowing cold. The old lady in the big blue hat followed me out; she reached over and touched me on the arm.

'That thing on your neck,' she said, in a thin, quavering voice, 'my late, dear husband had one in the fifties. Around the time the first sputnik destroyed the weather. I rubbed it with lard every night. That got rid of it. Try it. Try lard. Only the best lard, of course.' She turned and went back into the chapel.

Lard! What a stupid idea. I walked down the street to the bus stop, then turned round and went to the shop on the corner. I looked at the lard, smug in its tight white packets. I caught sight of my reflection in the shop window. The thing on my neck looked as big as a satsuma. I picked up a packet of lard and took it to the till.

'What's that thing on your neck?' the lad behind the counter said, as he put my lard in a carrier.

'Just give me the lard,' I said. 'Just give me the lard. Just give me the lard.'

There's Always a Man in a Cardigan

Lindsay sat up and said, 'I've started.' I sat up in bed and looked at the clock: 0101. It seemed more like a cry for help than a time. 'Are you sure?' I said, tentatively. I remembered the time two days before when I'd come home from school to find her holding on to the occasional table and trying to take her mind off things by watching Tony Hart make a mural out of sugar lumps. We'd dashed through Barnsley faster than the police did during the Ronald Biggs in Mexborough rumour, but when we got to the maternity unit it was a false alarm.

'I'm sure,' she said, 'get the car out, you're going to be a dad.' She came downstairs slowly, deliberately, her face occasionally twisting up with pain. I'd told her I was going to be there at the birth but now I wasn't so sure. I think really I'd have liked to pace about outside and then get called in to see a face in a shawl and start handing out cigars. For years I didn't know that I'd been born. My mam said the nurse had brought me through the snow. I asked why the nurse had to bring me, and my mam said she would have brought me herself but she was in bed poorly at the time. Later, when I was at junior school, Pud Stennett explained how babies were born. It was a rainy Saturday afternoon in 1965 in my auntie's shed and me and Pud had just tried to smoke some balsa wood cigarettes.

'You know breasts,' he said. Breasts. The word made me go red. He said it again. 'You know breasts.' 'Yes.' 'Well you know the bits at the end.'

'What bits?'

'Nittles.'

'Nittles?'

'Nittles. Women feed their babies through 'em. Well, that's how the babies are born. Through the nittles.'

'How do you mean?' The balsa wood smoke was starting to get to me. I felt a bit sick. Pud lowered his voice as though my Auntie might be standing outside the shed, listening.

'Well half the baby's born through one nittle and the other half's born through the other nittle and then the doctor sews you together and that's why you've got a belly button. It's where your halves were put together by a doctor.'

I was overwhelmed. I didn't know what to say. Then a sudden thought occurred to me.

'What about twins?' I asked. Stennett's voice was even softer now. 'I know but I can't tell thi.'

'I'll give thi all my spare civil war cards.'

Pud Stennett loved civil war cards, and I saw he couldn't resist my offer.

He leaned very close to me. His face looked old and wise in the stale balsa wood smoke.

'Four nittles,' he said.

I got the car out of the garage and Lindsay struggled in. It was a clear, crisp moonless night in December, and I could see my breath as I closed the garage door. Funny thing about Pud Stennett. He ended up teaching biology.

The car started first time and we were off. Lindsay sat in the back, me driving slowly, trying not to panic. It was only a few months since I'd passed my test and I still wasn't too confident. Lindsay leaned forward and said, 'You can try second gear if you want,' and I bit back a stinging reply.

My Auntie Elsie always used to say, 'Tell 'em about the jam when the fire's gone out' which apparently meant 'Always try to keep people's mind off things' so I said to Lindsay, 'Would you like some music on the 8-track? I've got Jethro Tull, Fairport Convention.' I was still into progressive in those days. She shook her head.

'Just try and drive a bit faster,' she said.

I got up to thirty miles an hour and said, 'I'll tell you what. I bet we see an old bloke in a cardigan walking a dog. I'll bet your first year's family allowance.' She didn't reply; she knew I was rambling.

It's been a theory of mine for years, that: The Old Bloke With The Cardigan and Dog Theory. It started when I was a sixth-former and I used to go to the Corner Pin on a Friday Night and get legless on two and a half pints of Barnsley Bitter. Me and my mates would stagger home after midnight and no matter what the weather was we always saw a wizened old bloke in a cardigan walking a dog. We'd have competitions: who'd be the first one to spot him? Would he be walking towards Barnsley up Kendray Hill or away from Barnsley towards Stairfoot? What colour would his cardigan be? Would it be buttoned? If so, how many buttons? And, the clincher: would he speak and if he spoke, what would he say? We had a points system: if he said 'Evening' or 'Goodnight', we got five points. If he was aggressive and said something like 'Get on ooam before I crack yer' or 'You college lads shouldn't be drinking mucky beer', we got ten points, but the crowning glory, if Barnsley FC had been playing that night, was if he said the immortal phrase 'How's Barnsley Gone On?' Thirty points. Magic!

We drove up the road, past the garden centre, through Ardsley and towards Barnsley. We still hadn't seen him and, funnily enough, I was really wanting to see him. While I was at college I'd worked the old man and the dog into a kind of folk-myth: he protected Barnsley, I'd say to open-gobbed lasses from the Home Counties; he's like the lamplighter, I'd say, the night watchman, the guardian angel of a dirty northern town. Then I'd turn slightly away and vomit spectacularly onto a pile of books that always contained *The Catcher in the Rye* and *The Great Gatsby*. The girls from the Home Counties would leave the room and I'd be alone with an engineer from Stockport called Miles. The rich are different from us.

We drove into the hospital grounds. I was going to park in the car park but Lindsay told me you were allowed to drive up to the door. At the door we were put in a lift, whisked to a ward, details were taken, efficient nurses bustled about, and I felt out of it. I'd got a joke ready. If they said, 'Do you want to be there at the birth?' I was going to say, 'Well, I was there at the conception so I may as well go for the double!' but nobody asked me.

A little nurse who looked like Roy Barraclough took Lindsay off to a room. 'I'd like to be there,' I said, quietly; 'We'll call you when we're ready, Mr Matthewman,' said Roy. I walked over to the window: Barnsley was laid out, orange and black under the stars. I tried to recognise individual streets and imagined blokes with dogs and cardigans on each one. I became suddenly, unaccountably, worried. My mate Trev at school, he's got three, and he told me I'd suffer from The Sudden Worry. 'Just before it's born, Richard, you'll be sure that it'll come out with three heads and more legs than a hockey team but you'll convince yourself that you'll still love it.' I hadn't believed it before, but now I could feel it creeping over me.

After a while a nurse came and said, 'You can go and see your wife now, Mr er… Matthewman.' She led me into a little room; Lindsay was dressed in a sort of smock, sitting on the bed. There was a portable telly in one corner and a couple of paperback books on a shelf.

They say it'll be a while yet; it could be the morning before anything happens,' she said.

I wandered over to the telly and switched it on. Son of Godzilla.

A dinosaur was just hatching out of an egg. Scientists watched, their lips mouthing furious Japanese, but sounding American; the dinosaur wobbled out of the bits of eggshell and stood unsteadily. I turned it off. The Sudden Worry returned. When ours was born it would look like a triceratops.

The room, like all hospital rooms, was red hot. It reminded me of afternoons in my grandad's greenhouse, listening to his chest rattling like waves over shingle. I was sweating. In the rush to get dressed I'd just pulled a sweater on with nothing underneath, so I couldn't even take it off. I said to Lindsay, 'Are you OK if I just pop outside for a minute, get some fresh air?' She just waved me away, being there at the birth was for my benefit, not hers. I noticed a door marked 'Waiting Room', and pushed it open slowly. It was pitch dark. I felt along the wall for the light switch and turned it on. There was a mass cry of 'GEEOR!' and I came face to face with half a dozen Barnsley dads-to-be who had been trying to sleep on the chairs, the tables, and in one case, the floor. They all sat, stunned in the harsh light, trying to rub their faces off the front of their heads. One man, although he was fully dressed, was casting about for his clothes and mumbling, 'Ah didn't think ah were on days this week. Ah didn't think I were on days.' A big man with an NCB jacket on said, 'What is it then doctor? A lad or a lass. If it's a lad she'll kill me. She reckons Friday nights makes lads.'

I went out. Not everybody wanted to be present at the birth. I needed to get out. I forgot about the toilet and went down in the lift and walked out into the freezing air. The sweat dried on my brow and I began to shiver. I was nervous. More than that, I was terrified. My old life was going to end, here, tonight, December 9th 1981, and a new life was going to begin with responsibilities and nappies and sleepless nights and a baby that looked like a triceratops. I had to be calm, had to be strong, for Lindsay's sake.

Then I identified the source of my worry, admitted it, faced up to it: I hadn't seen the bloke with the cardigan and the dog. Daft as it seemed, I needed to see him, needed something to link the old life to the new life in the freezing December air.

I walked through the car park to the hospital entrance. I looked up and down the road, quickly. Nobody. A black taxi zoomed past with an old lady sitting in the back clutching a handbag. Overhead, an aeroplane rumbled through the clear sky, its lights flashing. I needed to go back to Lindsay, but I needed to see the bloke with the dog. It was like when I was little and I had to do things in a certain order on Saturday Night: first, have my bath and hair wash, then sit downstairs on the settee with my jamas and dressing gown on watching Richard Baschart in *Voyage to the Bottom of the Sea*, eating a bag of plain crisps and keeping as many of them in my mouth as I could before I swallowed any.

Suddenly, just as I was about to give up and go back into the steaming hospital, I saw him; the man with the dog and the cardigan. I couldn't believe it. I walked down the road towards him, just to make sure he was real, and his little Jack Russell barked at me. He looked at me like I was mad, or drunk, or both. 'Evening,' he said. And I recognised him! It was Flour-on-Hands! He used to work at the tennis-ball factory and he used to delight in telling us students about all the times during the day he and his wife made love. 'I once came up behind her while she were baking scones,' he said, 'and we did it there and then over the sink, and she still had flour on her hands!' We christened him Flour-on-Hands after that, although we never called him that to his face, and seeing him now, this night of all nights, linked all my past and my future together in a way I couldn't fathom.

'Flour-on-Hands!' I said. I couldn't remember his real name.

'What the hell are you on about?' he said. The Jack Russell was growling now.

'Richard Matthewman, tennis-ball factory, 1975,' I said. 'My wife's having a baby in there…' and as I pointed to the hospital lit up like a great ocean liner, I realised that that's where I should be, with my future, not my past, and I ran across the car park like my shoes were on fire.

They were just taking Lindsay into the delivery suite when I dashed out of the lift. 'Where've you been?' she shouted. 'It's OK, I've seen the man with the cardigan and the dog,' I said, but I knew she wasn't listening and I followed her into the room where new life began.

Just Like Ours Except for the Ducks

The man paid for the taxi in bags of ten pence coins. Ten quid in bags of ten pence coins and the driver never blinked. The man lugged his bag into the travel centre and bought a single to Cleethorpes. 'Eight quid,' said the ticket man. The ticket man needed a shave. The man took out his bags of ten pences.

On the platform the man stood in front of a chocolate machine and spoke to it in a loud voice. He said Give me your bastard chocolate. Nothing happened. He patted the ticket in his pocket. Then he patted it again. Then he slapped his pocket, then he thumped it hard. The ticket was still there.

On the train, the man seemed to relax. He looked out at the flat fields in the wasteland near Thorne. He tried to think.

Cleethorpes would be wonderful. The family would meet him. The two girls, pretty as pictures in their blue dresses. The little boy, he's a little rogue, walking now, straining against his reins. Shouting Daddy, maybe. Maybe all of them shouting Daddy and dancing a bastard jig. Maybe.

And the wife. The lovely wife, standing open armed. Smiling the kind of smile you dream about.

They would walk through Cleethorpes along the front and the children would say Daddy Daddy can we have this and can we have that and it would be as though the words were coming out of their mouths in little balloons like the balloons you see in comics. The words would hang in the air for him to hear and there would be no need to look at the words and make them out slowly and painfully. That would be lovely. And yes they could have that and yes they could have this. And out would come the bags of ten pences and there would be laughing and shouting and the little lad straining at his reins and the wife smiling her big smile and saying He's my man. Me and him, we're like this.

The train rolled into Scunthorpe and the man smiled. He knew one or two jokes about Scunthorpe. Really funny ones. Bastard killers. He'd tell them to the children, as they walked round Cleethorpes. The sun has got his bastard hat on. And they'd all laugh till they cried and the wife would smile her big smile and the sun would shine and make them sweat.

Outside Barnetby the train stopped. It sat there, humming. The passengers stared out at clumps of trees and at a distant farmhouse. The sun beat down and people used newspapers and books to fan themselves. The driver climbed out of the train and stood talking into a telephone by the line. The man looked out of the window. This is not good is it? he said. This is not bastard good at all. The woman opposite looked at her copy of the *People's Friend*. Lends your paper, the man said. Lends it. The woman hurriedly gave him the paper. He looked at it and gave it her back. I've read that one, he said. It's next week's. Then he laughed.

He got up and walked down the train with his bag full of the bags of ten pences. The train was almost empty. It sat there in the heat. This is not good, he said. Then the train set off, and continued by the squares of yellow rape.

After they had walked along the front they would go to the caravan. The kiddies would be tired but happy. They would clutch in their hot hands the things he had bought them from his bags of ten pences. From his bags of ten pences and I bet the odd Irish one and it doesn't matter when the sun shines out of a bastard clear blue sky. The kids would fall asleep and their little eyes would shut and they would look so peaceful. And the wife would smile her big smile and they would go in the end bedroom and the walls would bastard drip.

After that there would be the rest of their lives, like a tree. Like the tree he used to see, changing with the seasons, growing bigger and bigger, blocking out more light. More and more light. Some great jokes about Scunthorpe.

That had been the first of the ten pences. He had broken into the bag, broken into it to ring the house. And nobody in. So he had rung his mother, and she had told him about Cleethorpes and the van. And the children. And wouldn't it be better if. And he had said Just you tell them to meet me and he had slammed the phone down and the sow never knew bastard nothing anyway. Never made no bastard sense at all.

Not far now. Big chemical works at Immingham pumping out shit. None of your bastard shit must fall on the heads of my kiddies.

They would stand there, waving. All three kiddies and the little one straining at his reins. And the bags full of the ten pences in all the slots and the lights flashing and their little fists full of bastard belm.

The train rattled into Grimsby. Not far now, you ugly fat bastard, he said to a man walking past the train. Not far now.

He remembered what his mate had said. The mate who had been so close. The mate who read science fiction all the time until the lads said he was on bastard Mars all the time and the mate said No I'm not on Mars because there's no atmosphere there not like in this shitty hole.

Anyway the mate had said that he'd read a story about a bloke who said that there was a parallel world to this one and in this world everything was the same except that people walked about with ducks on their heads.

And the man had said Bastard ducks what are you about bastard ducks. And the mate, who was a bloody clever bloke, had said There is, according to this story, a parallel world where people walk about with ducks on their heads and it might be true it might not be bastard science fiction.

And the man had said That's rubbish that is pal, but secretly he took notice because the bloke was a clever bloke. Mind you he couldn't have been that clever or they wouldn't have caught him.

The train rolled into Cleethorpes station, and they would be there to meet him and the little one would strain at his reins and the girls in their dresses pretty as pictures and the wife smiling her big smile. He knew some really great jokes about Scunthorpe to make them smile and they would be waiting for him on the station.

The man got off the train and looked down the platform. There is this parallel world where the people are just like us except that they walk about with ducks on their heads. Some really great jokes about Scunthorpe.

On the Closure of Cadeby Colliery

'At first I heard a kind
of scrambling noise

then I heard a fluttering
and there was a bird

squeeze through, somehow,
the gas fire, the actual

gas fire, flapping about
behind the fireguard.

Your dad
was in the kitchen and…'

    I thought of how
    when the train stopped at Conisbrough Station
    you looked right and saw
    two lots of winding gear,
    how you looked left and saw
    two men demolishing Conisbrough Station.

    Oh and then I thought of how
    my dad worked on a farm in Lanarkshire
    and it was the 1930s and he joined
    the navy, and he saw flying fish
    'looking like bird and fish joined'
    and he'd seen nothing like it in Lanarkshire.

'…I ran in there with the kids and
anyway, he went home and

brought his landing net,
caught it, let it

go in the garden.
A bird in a landing net!'

Title (Northumberland June 11th/12th 1987)

Just notes really.
Nothing like real writing.

Profit is unpaid wages
The boys ran into the trees.

The girls cried.
Redraft the sand.
What is dad doing with

his shadow on the sand?
There is a new sign,
a footpath sign.
frightened, bud.
Redraft me, I am

Elizabeth holds up a cassette, spools
it out. 'I'm bandaging
the moon

Polling station.
Crowds of old people.
Lesbury village.

A Conservative landrover
with a flag flying
roaring through the streets
of Alnwick.

You are weeping Robin Day
weeping Peter Snow
And yes you are

Three a.m. The foghorn.
The day redrafting itself.

The Flag

How do you paint te

rror?

Slow Thaw

My daughter tells me
of a dream she had.
'You were standing there.'

What was I saying?
'Nothing.' What was I doing?
'Nothing.' Where was I?

'I had a dream.'
She stands at the window
looking out at the white

garden, at the footprints
that begin at the hedge
and go nowhere.

After a week of grey
the sky stretches blue
to breaking point.

She has forgotten the dream.
She shows me a painting
of someone in black.

And who is this? I ask,
pointing to a blue lump,
several red lines

in a corner. 'That's scribble'
she says, 'just scribble'
looking at me

as if I should know.

In Fear of Abstraction

The guard is small,
smaller than me.
'There's a failure
in front of us.
We don't know
when they'll move him'

he says. I stare
into the night,
into the night.
When I was small
I used to go into
the garden, saying

'I'm going to think'
and I used to walk
around the garden
in circles. Look:
an aeroplane,
low over Stockport,

small in the dark.
I've got a photo at home
of me when I was small,
laughing my bloody head off.
It's dark outside.
Down the train

the guard picks up
a small green shoe.
Look at the sky:
the aeroplane circling
around the dark,
into the dark.

Brief Encounter

He stood on the platform, and waved
at the disappearing words. I mean

he waved at the disappearing train.
A hand waved back from the words,

from the train I mean. He walked
into the cafe, into the room

where they had shared so much:
words (should I say, coffee) and words

(I mean food). His train waited on
the words or should I say his train

waited on the rails. He lingered
over his words, and a waiter

hovered, expecting payment, because
nobody had told him that words were free
or that they should be.

The Day after Armistice Day

Two men are jogging
in early morning light
by a canal.

I imagine
they are both
called Doreen,

which may seem
irrelevant,
but my memory

is locking
(with a click
audible

to the other passengers
on this crowded train)
into Doreen Parry

who keeps a shop
in Darfield
where I once bought a toy shotgun

for 8/11d.
So this is a poem
about disarmament,

not about jogging men
called Doreen.
Fooled you.

The Mirror in the Toilet

Some pieces are sharp
and some pieces
are very sharp. I've got
my hand in the toilet
and the water is freezing,
nearly frozen, and

there are bits of white
Andrex, little rolled bits,
among the sharp bits,
piling them on the frame

of the mirror. I just
walked out of the bathroom,
shut the door,
and the mirror fell off,
smashed in the toilet.
The water is so cold

that I have to stop and dry
my hands on an old
blue towel. I check my hands
for blood or splinters.
I hold them up to the light
and look at them, closely.

Essential Engineering Works

The train stops somewhere in the lit
midlands, sun reflecting... you know
the kind of thing I mean. The lit

midlands. Let me tell you some things
about this poem. This poem happens
on a train stopped in the midlands,

and this poem also happens, if a poem
can happen, in a gallery in Wales,
where a man is looking at photographs.

The two parts of this poem happen at once,
quickly, like the snap of a successful
christmas cracker. I am sorry; this poem

was meant to move more quickly to the
gallery in Wales from the lit midlands.
It is stuck on the line

somewhere between the midlands and Wales.
Listen, you can hear the poem's engine
running. It will start soon, it will

lurch into life. Essential engineering works
are holding the poem still; a man
is standing before a photograph, and he

is seeing only himself in the glass.
Listen, hear the poem's engine running.
Gaze at the photograph and wait, wait.

The er Barnsley Seascapes

1. *Goldthorpe er Seascape*

Park the car. Wind
the window down. Listen.
Shanties echoing
up the tight street

as the pitmen sing
their way from work.
The YTS lamplighter
stands, and his matches

cough out in
the well-trained wind.
He was not a clever
boy at school

so all he can say is
shit, not like us
clever people, who wind
the window down to catch

the dying tradition
on our Japanese tape recorders.
Shanties, clinking like
cardboard money,

the cardboard money
they have round here.
Burns easier.
Cheaper than coal.

2. *M1 Seascape near Hoyland: er it's a rough day*

They huddle in their coats
and the gaffer holds his gun
but only for effect. For this
photograph I am taking, I suppose.

For the interview, the gaffer
is proud: 'We have only six more
miles of motorway to roll up
and dump in the sea' he quips.

3. *er Darfield Seascape*

And the waves pound
against Clifton's shop
and Clifton's shop never closes.
On Christmas Day someone rushes in
for a pair of tights. She has
a bulging purse from Habitat
in the shape of a bath
filled with coal. Habitat coal,
silly bastard. Put it this way:
Darfield was mentioned in the Domesday Book.
Put it like this: a passing mention,
more of a mutter.

4. *Little Houghton Seascape er like*

British Coal
sold the houses

made us live
in heads.

Great big
severed heads.

Rows of heads
overlooking the sea.

Sometimes I stand
in the eyes

and I cry.
Then I burn

the tears.
Cheaper than coal.

5. *An Old Seadog er Speaks*

First it was called NCB, you'd see it
on the boats, then British Coal, on
the wharves, then they changed the name
to British A Vase of Flowers, changed all
the boats, all the wharves, all the
signs outside the pits, then they
changed it to British Very Nice
and a month later to British Smile
and they kept repainting the boats
the wharves the fish the seaweed the

6. *er from a Learned Paper about Seascapes*

Very few of er the South Yorkshire
Coastal Mining Settlements survive
in anything like their original

er state. Some have become islands,
some have sunk into the sea, some
have worked loose from the earth

and slither around the countryside
scaring er owls and other woodland
creatures. One was found in Harrogate,

a town in North Yorkshire next to
the sea. 'It had er wings' said a local,
'and was tired from much hard flying'

7. Seaview Video, Barnsley: Er Latest Offers

Barnsley is Basingstoke!	£1.00 a night
Barnsley is Basingstoke 2!	£1.00 a night
The Cruel Sea (Remake)	£1.00 a night
Lost Horizon (Remake)	£1.00 a night
Barnsley is Japan!	£1.00 a night
Barnsley is Japan 2!	£1.00 a night

8. Seascape Could er Be Anywhere around here

Only the water, solid
and glinting. Only
the noise of the water,

and the noise of the moon
slowly deflating, and
only the noise of the stars

being sold, clinking,
keeps me awake
all day.

The Christmas Tree's Press Conference

No. I can't
reveal too much.

All storms are terrible.
This one, I agree,
was more terrible than most.

Yes, the baubles
suffered damage.

Yes, the angel
was lost.

No.

Gentleman at the back?

No. No, the tinsel
has always been this colour.

Don't

you like this colour?
Don't you like this colour?

Bastard? Shall I come over there
and kick shit out of you?

Bastard.

Sorry. I'm sorry.
It takes… a lot
out of one.

'The movement of the sea,
The deep, the deep,
    Holding you and me,
The deep'

as Belloc wrote.

The Grimness: BBC Radio 4, Tuesday, 8.30 p.m.

We don't talk much
but when we talk
we talk about the Grimness.

Almost a cliché
in this muck.
Ah, The Grimness.
I remember it well.

And now on Radio 4
the poet Ian McMillan
presents a feature
on the Grimness of 1993
and what it did.

He talks to a number of people
who survived it
and some who
didn't.

Such a big microphone.

It just sort of sat there
on the settee.
Occasionally it looked at
the coffee table.
Sometimes it glanced
at a wedding photo.
Not its own.
Any wedding photo.
It
had
sacks
full.

Can you tell me something
anything about the Grimness.

Look at the view, kid.
Grimethorpe. The band
playing their lips out
but you can't hear them
because the window's shut.
It's smashed but at least it's
shut.

Grimethorpe. Is that mike on?
Is that thing turning?
You can't shift for Channel 4
film crews round here. Big fat bastards
with the arse crack showing, lugging
cameras. Thin kids with boom mics.

You pick up the lingo.

Little lasses with clipboards.
The colliery band rushing
from shoot to shoot.

But the Grimness.
Can we talk about the Grimness?

In the sky, look. That constellation
there.
Round here we call it Wrecked Oil
Tanker,
that constellation, because there's no
shape
to it and it's black all around it.

Is that thing turning?
That's a joke.

O pinpoint the Grimness for me madam.
Pointpin it. Speak into this thing.
This, call it what you like, pimple.
Speak faster than you normally would
to compensate for my dying battery.
And in a higher register than you
would normally employ. Pin pin
the Grim? Point it?

The Grimness? Not a bad pub.
Dead tap room. Old caps with blokes under.
Knock of a domino echoing back from the '26 strike.
Scab's knock, you see. We pretended we didn't hear it.
It flies round the tap room like a bat. Nice lounge,
young people get in it. Just the one hairstyle
between them. They pass it round like drugs.
Big stuffed fish on the wall. Most pubs have a
big stuffed fish on the wall. Look at that one.
Look closely. Not a fish at all. Look.
A bird

in the shape of a fish. We're not daft.

There we have it. The Grimness. Grimethorpe 1993.
Defined. A miasma. The sticky bit of an envelope.
A burst h.w. bottle. Nelson: kiss me, Grimey.
Distant piccolo music. An ant's first breath.
Hooks in a butcher's trousers. I have polished my shoes.
Al Pacino in Carry On Grimethorpe. Valves. Sellotape.
Jiffy bag with a broken hen in it. Ten to four in the morning.

The Miner's Breakfast:

A bowl of Grimethorpe flakes. Look: a free model of Thunderbird
8, the forgotten one, like Ghandi, the tenth Marx Brother.

That's a short shopping list mister!
It's okay!
No shops!

Ian McMillan. BBC Radio 4. Grimethorpe.

Was that okay? Was my voice concerned enough? Enough about
the Grimness? To be honest I wanted to laugh most of the time.
It's funny. Do you think I should do that bit at the end again?
Let's listen back. A man was trying to breathe in a house two miles
away. Bloody deafened me pal.

Modernism: The Umbrella Girl Forgets What She is Talking About

'The manufacture of Umbrella Frames and Tubes at Stocksbridge
occupies... 300 workers, a majority of whom are girls... the finishing
department is quite a speciality of the gentler sex.' (C. H. Bird-David,
1910)

I'm talking about umbrellas.

I gitted, mainly. Summer afternoons I gitted,
until they put me on the ferrules
or the pinning in. Ivy gitted too,
and Florence, and Olive, and Nellie.

Hannah was on the japanning. The lacquer
stained her hands terrible. A man with
a dirty face is talking to a man
with a clean face. The taxi firm

is two doors away. I envy your fluidity.
The bodging was the worst. You had to
knock the lacquer out of the holes
in the ribs. They give you offalls,

little leather caps to put on your
finger and thumb to save them
while you pressed the ribs
to test for strength. I think

I'd rather have a lion tear me to death
than a snake. I made a snake out of
plasticene. It crawled up my arm. Like eels.
When he brought eels I always said

Take them eels to Jimmy Hancock.

We are talking about eels.

Burst Pipe with 'A Level' Notes

Here I am, carrying   Narrator?
this empty kettle through a clear   Persona?
December night,   Winter of the Soul?

My Dad a few yards behind,   God/Christ?
my wife at home, mopping,   Madonna?
looking at the water   Sense of making whole?

coming through the ceiling.   Virgin birth?
That blinking red eye   Drink?
of the aeroplane   Idea of Heaven?

We see every night at this time   Eternity?
and that girl   Made-up?
with the made-up face   Pun on Fiction?

collecting the Avon
catalogues. Ding Dong.
Face framed in the door.

Every time I ring
the plumber's mobile phone
he doesn't answer it.

When he left our house
he said he was going
to look into a loft.

I fill the kettle
at my mother's. She gives
me some bacon.

Scavenger?
Doorbell?
Like a portrait?

Prayer?
Plumber = God?
Church and state?

Desertion by God?
Looking into darkness?
Severed head?

Family life?
Bacon?
Is God dead?

Halifax!

History nags like a mouth
ulcer, and you can't tell
where one year starts
and the other one ends

except the slang gets
further away from words
you understand. Hunk,
dish, pillock you grew

up with, streets of them.
Now bevs pull bleeds
and you shout Halifax!
I made that last one up.

History nags like a mouth
bleeding, a dream
you can't remember
and therefore never had,

a film you never saw
but read the reviews of
and they were all bad,
they were all bad.

Halifax! History nags
like a mouth, History smells
like a DSS-approved hotel,
a waiter with a tie on elastic,

a receptionist drinking
lager through a straw
who tells you No Messages
Halifax! I'm on this late

night bus, alone except for
a hunk, a dish and a pillock
with a mouth ulcer, throbbing
like history with batteries.

It's my stop. I'll get off.
Invent some new slang. Halifax
Canvey! Oban! Barnsley!
Dursley! Chester le Street!

Rotherham

Rotherham's always been an exotic place to me. I live near
Barnsley, about six miles from here, and before the invention of
the M1 we used to drive through Rotherham on empty Sunday
afternoons to visit my Auntie Mabel on the outskirts of Clowne.
We'd drive through impossibly unworldly places like Greasbrough,
Halfway and Swallownest. There's a street in Greasbrough called
Harold Croft and I knew a man in Barnsley called Harold Croft.
Impossible, unworldly. It's a little terrace just down the hill from
the taxidermist. My dad would sing 'Roll Along Covered Wagon
Roll Along', my brother would be asleep with his head lolling,
and my mother would be checking her face in the vanity mirror.
That was then, this is now. I'm in Rotherham trying to forget
my cosy 1960s pictures of the place, and trying to find some 90s
images. Here's one: the discarded rubber band on the floor. They're
everywhere, not just in Rotherham. Britain is covered in rubber
bands. We know they're really dropped by postmen, but they're
sinister. They're rubber bands from the sky, bendy shapes from
hell, people turned into rubber bands when we're not looking.
Harold Croft: street in Greasbrough, man in Barnsley, rubber
band near Rotherham Library. Here's another image, wrapped
round this fence near Rotherham central station: the wrecked
cassette, the tape flapping in the wind. You see them everywhere:
hanging from trees, waving from barbed wire fences, coiling
along the floor beside a couple of rubber bands. Is this it, then
for Rotherham? For the North? From travel through uncharted
parts called Halfway to a bit of rubbish on a mucky floor? By
Rotherham Central Station I sat down and wept? We once came
on a school trip to Rotherham when I was an infant. Sixty of
us on one Burrows Bus, still dusty from taking the early shift to
Darfield Main. All the way, people kept saying, 'Watch out for
that Lion, he'll have thi.' I had lettuce sandwiches with salad
cream and I was worried because Peter Wake had said, 'Lions Like
Lettuce'; I knew really that there weren't any Lions in Rotherham
because I'd looked for them on my way back from Auntie Mabel's
the week before and not seen any. We walked into Clifton Park
museum and there, in the entrance, was the biggest lion I'd ever
seen. Stuffed, one paw aloft. I wept, and held Mrs Hinchcliffe's

hand tight. The bus driver, Biv Burrows, walked up to the glass and tapped it boldly. 'It's okay, kid,' he said, 'I think it's dead.' The lion's still there. Go and see it next time you're in Rotherham. And Peter Wake was wrong: it doesn't like lettuce, it likes rubber bands and cassette tape. Don't be frightened. I think it's dead.

Snails on the West Shore, August 1991

It had been raining, and my son
wanted to see the snails. We ran
out of the guesthouse, long before breakfast,

our feet brushing the owner's *Telegraph*
in the hall where the paperboy had left it,
almost stepped on the face of John McCarthy,

blinking in the light of the world's flash,
and we ran towards the Gogarth Abbey Hotel
where Alice Liddell stayed as a little girl,

Alice in Wonderland waiting inside her
like the idea of a butterfly waits inside
a picture of a caterpillar. My son

did his usual trick, running like mad
at a gang of gulls, laughing as they
climbed the sky, landed on the roof

of the Gogarth Abbey Hotel. Then we began
to see the snails, far more than yesterday,
dozens of them, punctuating the damp path

like they owned it, slowly, so slowly,
from the wall to the road. My son
stopped, his three-year-old head

focusing down to the snails moving slow
as the low clouds that hung over the Orme.
He stared at the snails, the slow old man

inside him waiting like the idea of a bird
waits inside the picture of an egg. Down past
the Gogarth Abbey Hotel a gull swooped down

on a snail, bashed it on the floor, rose
towards the Orme's clouds and the grey sky.
My son was frightened, looked down

at the snails crossing the path, looked up
at the gulls slicing the sky's silence, looked
at me, saw the boy I once was, the slow

old man I would become, crossing paths
in a grey winter. Later, in the residents'
lounge, he laid his cars out in a long line;

'Is it a traffic jam?' I asked. 'It's snails
crossing the path,' he said. I bent down
to pick one of the cars up. 'Leave it,'

he said, 'It's a snail crossing the path.'
I looked up, saw John McCarthy on the tv,
blinking in the light of the world's flash,

thought of how we must learn to live together;
snails, young boys, fathers, and the slow
old men they must become, under the Great Orme

and the clouds dark as a cell door.

Three Boring Miles on the Exercise Bike

Three boring miles. The television flickering
in the corner of my eye. A man talking.

The view doesn't alter, of course. The rain
coming down steadily, Joe's grandma

taking him down to school, coming back again.
Mile one. The speedometer hovering

around twelve. So in an hour I could be
almost in Sheffield, halfway to Leeds,

my legs going slowly, slowly, going nowhere,
my wife lifting the same cup of coffee

to her lips for mile after mile, the steam
pulling away from the cup like smoke,

a man talking. It's me, saying the same things
over and over again. Mile two. The phone rings,

I pedal, my wife answers it again and again.
It's the same bad news, pulling away like smoke,

Joe's grandma taking him to school.
She waves this time. She waved last time.

Her glasses are the same as they have been for years.
My view doesn't change. A window of trees,

rain, Joe's grandma, my wife, the cup of coffee,
the telephone, the bad news, my legs going slowly,

slowly, in an hour I could be halfway to here,
almost into this room, the room pulling away

like smoke from a dying fire. Mile three.
The view doesn't alter. A man talking. It's me.

Smoke

It started with a dream:
she wore smoke, she wore a wide skirt,
she was a slow dancer, lived in the North
she

and it continued with a walk,
early Sunday morning, to get out
of the house that pressed
like a flannel. Like a flannel
on a mask.

Smoke. Grey smoke from
a burning chimney
in a smokeless pit village.

The dream:
I look good in blue, like the sea.
I look good in black, like the night.

I dream poems. When I try
to write them they are just

smoke. Time cracked. March
in Summer, Christmas a long
cool drink with a slice of lemon.

I think that's what the dream said.
I scribbled it down in the dark.

Anyway, how does the blind man know
when his paper is dirty?

If you see what I mean.

Bosnia Festival: Your Full Guide by our Arts Reporter

At 10.00 a.m. mime show
by The Shuffling Headscarves.
Nothing much happens;
some shuffling, weeping.
Mimed weeping, that is.

At Midday, cabaret
in The Bread Queue
by The Arguing Headscarves.
Nothing much happens;
a feeble argument. Behind them
The Ducking Headscarves
are ducking the snipers.
The Shuffling Headscarves
mime weeping.

At three p.m. a one man show
by a man in a white suit
talking into a camera.
Nothing much happens.
The Shuffling Headscarves, The
Arguing Headscarves and the Ducking
Headscarves continue their act

which one critic described
as a lot of shuffling, arguing
and ducking.

There's so much happening.
There's almost too much to take in.
A kind of festival fatigue
comes over you: all these headscarves,
all that weeping, all those gestures.
Godot turned up last night, by the way,
in a headscarf, weeping.

The actors stood with their mouths open
like fish. Fish on a bloody slab.

The 70

The 70. What a wonderful bus that was; Sheffield to Upton. I
never went as far as Upton (did anybody?) but I often went from
Darfield to Sheffield and back, to Pink Floyd concerts at the City
Hall, to the Cineplex to see *The Life and Times of Judge Roy Bean*,
to the bookshops on Chapel Walk. A whole cultural education
defined from the top deck of a bus that seemed to turn every
corner, go down every side street, and wait unaccountably at
Wombwell Baths for ages.

The route: 'I'd get on at Darfield Ring. It would be the early
70s, say 1972. The Darfield Urban District Council men would
be putting plants in the middle of the roundabout. One of
them would be sucking a tomato. He always sucked a tomato.
Up Nanny Marr Road, down Snape Hill Road, past Low Valley
Juniors, my old school, past Darfield Main and into Wombwell. A
lot got off in Wombwell, especially if it was Market Day. I wished
that I could get off and run to Grace's van for an ice-cream, but
there was never time. Then up to Wombwell Baths where my
dad would take me on a Saturday morning to teach me to swim.
He didn't succeed. The long wait. Sometimes the driver switched
the engine off. Kids with towels and wet hair would get on and
sit there shivering. Then up Hough Lane and instead of going
up Wood Walk we'd turn left; one hour we'd turn left and go to
Hemingfield, other hours we'd turn left and go into Jump. ('Is
this bus going to Jump? Well hold it down while I get on.') Then
the indefinable lanes around Hoyland and Elsecar, chugging up
and down hills past pubs, schools, shops, more pubs. Past the
NCB Workshops at Elsecar. We didn't know that in twenty years
the NCB Workshops at Elsecar were going to be the centre of
Barnsley's burgeoning tourist industry. We weren't that clever.
Down into Chapeltown. A lot on, a lot off. Another wait. Then
up the hill towards Ecclesfield and the cruel trick that your
brain always played was that you thought you were almost there;
you'd left the Barnsley pits (Darfield Main, the recently closed
Wombwell Main, Elsecar, Barrow, the one at Platts Common,
Smithy Wood) behind and you were entering the Metropolis. You
weren't. Through Ecclesfield. Past an optician's. Past a club called
the Limes. To Lane Top. Down towards the Wicker. Almost there

now. The windows would be steamed up and you'd be feeling a bit bilious. Then into Pond Street, and off to the City Hall, the Pictures, the Bookshops.

I still can't drive, and I sometimes catch the 70 into Wombwell from Darfield. Except it's not called the 70 anymore, it's the 271, and it's not a huge double decker, it's a little minibus called a Town Link. I don't think it's possible to get from Sheffield to Upton anymore by public transport without an overnight stay. Maybe I'll try it sometime.

Frog Dream

great moon, hopping
sky: pond
great moon
like the time before legs
great moon
rolling at memory's
pond edge
great moon, singing
croaking in the froglight
huge frog's head
hanging in the sky

Dear Mr McMillan

Dear Mr McMillan,
My cousin tells me that you are the writer of a humorous column in the *Sheffield Telegraph*. I wonder if you would be interested in hearing about a funny thing that happened to me in June of 1963? I myself have not read your column but I used to enjoy Cassandra in the *Daily Mirror*.

Yours sincerely, Mr A B of Gleadless.

Dear Mr A B,
Many thanks for your letter. Yes, I'd love to hear about the funny thing that happened to you in 1963. I'm always looking for material for my column. I'm too young to remember Cassandra myself!

All the best, Ian McMillan.

Dear Mr McMillan,
As requested I am writing with details of the incident that happened to me in 1963, in the hope that it will be of interest and amusement to your readers. It took place on the evening of June 4, as my wife and I were enjoying a quiet evening at home. I was boiling the kettle for the Ovaltine when I heard my wife shout from the front room. I went into the front room and there to my surprise I was greeted by the very humorous sight of my wife sitting on the floor with a small to medium pile of soil on her head. What had happened was that my wife was standing on a stool (or a chair, I forgot which) to put a potted plant on a high shelf on our display unit and had slipped from the stool (or chair) thus bringing the plant pot onto her head. Well I can tell you we had a good laugh about it.

Yours sincerely, Mr A B of Gleadless.

Dear Mr A B,
Many thanks for sending me the story of the plant pot falling on your wife's head. Although it made me smile a bit, I don't know if it would be funny enough for my readers who are used to a pretty side-splitting standard! Perhaps you could tell me some more funny stories from your life?

All the best, Ian McMillan.

Dear Mr McMillan,
I was most disappointed to learn that you will not be able to use the funny story of the plant pot falling on my wife's head because it is not funny enough for your readers. I can assure you that my wife and I have laughed about it for many years now, on and off. Mind you, I did send it to Cassandra in 1966, and heard no more about it, despite SAE. Perhaps your readers will be interested in a remarkable coincidence that happened to me in 1973?

Yours sincerely, Mr A B of Gleadless.

Dear Mr A B,
Yes, please do send me details of the remarkable coincidence.

All the best, Ian McMillan.

Dear Mr McMillan,
As requested I am sending you details of the remarkable coincidence that happened to me in 1973. Every year my wife and I have a week in Cleethorpes at the Sea View Guest House. You can imagine my surprise when in 1973 the couple at the next table, a haulage contractor and his wife, were called Mr and Mrs Gleadless! I trust that this amazing but true coincidence will amuse and interest your readers. If you don't want to use it, throw it away. I sent it to Cassandra in 1974 but he said that he lost it.

Yours sincerely, A B of Gleadless.

A Cliché Defines the Moment
in a Poem about Language and Oppression

A blackened Yorkshire pit village
in the smoke
of a burning chimney, 1968;

Joan always burned her chimney
Sunday Mornings,
heating the oven for the Yorkshires.

'Yorkshire's finest Yorkshires!'
cried Joan, a pinny
on legs. Her husband George

smiled and smiled,
cracking his blue scars, and said
'You've hit the nail on the head!'

Outside, tall Sarah
and her husband Sam
new from Ayrshire, and a
pit shut as a cellar door,
listening at the window,
pulled to Yorkshire
by the NCB's smiling promises
and a film called *King Coal.*

Rows of houses like rows of boots.

Sarah leaned towards
the open window,
caught the end of the phrase
'...nail on the head!'
and smiled and smiled and said
'It's okay, Sam; they use clichés like we do'
and Sam leaned in the open window
like a sailor through a porthole and said
'You've hit the nail on the head!'

And they all smiled, like skulls smile.

Mining Town

As he goes to sleep
my son's face loses definition.
He becomes like the Man
in the Moon, or a child's
drawing of a face.

His eyes flicker. Outside, in
the light of a Summer evening
Mr Johnson bends down, picks leaves up,
only really he's looking for his wife
who died at the start of the year.

If I think hard I can recall her face just.
My daughters are talking about their visit
to the Yorkshire Mining Museum.
They went right to the face. It was
like a child's drawing
of a moonless night.

And that's it, really. This place
has gone down like a balloon,
one of those balloons that you find
behind the settee two weeks after Christmas.

Nothing more to say. I find it hard
to imagine my dad as a boxing champ;
he was, though, in the Navy, in the 1940s.
He's so gentle. I imagine him saying sorry
every time he punched somebody.

'I never went for the face'
he told me once.

A Discussion on Modern Poetry with Example: Postman Pat's Suicide Note

1

I like Blanka best, the way
he electrifies all the others.
Chun-Li is pretty good
and her Spinning Bird Kick

is astonishing, especially
in the six-button arcade version
like the one we played
on the Ferry. E. Honda

is good, too; we call him
Fat Eddie. He moves fairly
slowly, though, and his fat
never wobbles. Dhalsim's arms

and legs make me gasp, the way
they elongate. Ryu is deep.

2

Up and down the same hills
through the same weather
over and over, and that tune
only in my head
not in Ted Glen's.

All the birds are singing
and the day is just
the day.

Bar Wars

Pull up a comfortable chair, friend. Thrown another burn-effect log on the log-effect fire, and I'll tell you a story. A story of human endeavour and passion, of cunning and stealth. A story of sign-writing. I call the story Bar Wars, and I'm hoping to sell it to a Hollywood producer for a 27-figure sum. I've changed all the names to protect the innocent.

It all started a few months ago on the busy main road near our house. The road is dead straight, they told us at school it was Roman, and there are two big lay-bys within a few hundred yards of each other at the same side of the road.

One day, a caravan appeared in one of the lay-bys. A small touring caravan behind a Volvo estate. On the caravan were the words SNACK BAR and TEAS. It said JANET'S on the front, and on the back, for some reason, it said HOT N COLD. For a couple of days nothing happened because they're mighty suspicious folk round these parts. Then I began to notice the occasional car parked up, the odd truck. Inside the cab of the truck I would see a huge man making short work of a bacon sandwich the size of Rutland. I peeped into the caravan a few days later as I passed the full lay-by. Janet herself presided over a table surrounded by truckers, reps, and mysterious chaps who might have been spies. Janet rang a noisy till and slept easily in her bed, her dreams full of gently sizzling sausages and vehicles slowing down and coming to a halt.

Christmas approached. A man needs a good breakfast inside him. Janet added the word BREAKFASTS to the side of the little caravan and men queued at the door, lorries hooted as they went by, and Janet's name was famous from Dover to Wick. Janet put a tiny Christmas tree in the window of the caravan and on Christmas Eve all the truckers and reps and mystery men got a free mince pie with their whopping breakfasts.

The year turned into a new decade and Janet's trade stayed steady. Then the unthinkable happened: a rival caravan parked in the next lay-by. A lugubrious bloke with a face like a comic's straight man stood on a set of rickety steps and wrote on the caravan in thick black felt tip: TURNER'S TEA BAR. It took him days.

Janet shrugged him off. Her lay-by stayed full. Turner sat in his caravan, looking like a bereaved basset hound, gazing at the cars and lorries and vans and trucks zooming by to Janet's home comforts. Then Turner hit on a new strategy: signs at the side of the road. I pictured him in my mind's clear eye sitting bolt upright in bed and shouting: 'SIGNS AT THE SIDE OF THE ROAD!' He put two up, one at either side of the road, quite near his lay-by. TURNER'S TEA BAR, they read, NEXT LAY-BY. And he began to get customers. The odd one or two, to start with. Then three, and four. Where before Janet had eight customers and Turner had none, it became Janet six, Turner two; then Janet four, Turner four, and once or twice four-all. So Janet fought back: fire with fire. Two signs, at the side of the road, just in front of Turner's: JANET'S BREAKFASTS. And two cunning signs a good half mile before the lay-bys: JANET'S BREAKFASTS.

Turner wasn't going to take this lying down. No siree. Two more signs, a mile away from the lay-bys: TURNER'S TEA BAR, ONE MILE.

That was last week. It's neck and neck, no quarter asked, none given. It's a fight to the death. The market will only stand so much; there are only so many breakfasts a man can eat. And now the pub down the road is displaying a sign: BREAKFAST FROM 5AM. Watch out for a bleary-eyed spring on the old Roman road.

Sonny Boy Williamson is Trying to Cook a Rabbit in a Kettle

Ingredients:

1. Rabbit
2. Water

Method:

1. Attempt to get lid off kettle.
2. Attempt to get lid off kettle.
3. Attempt to put rabbit in kettle.
4. Use harmonica to squeeze rabbit in kettle.
5. Switch kettle on.
6. Settle down to watch *My Friend Flicka* on huge black and white 1960s hotel TV.
7. Inspect kettle. Trouser press switched on by mistake.
8. Take toast out of trouser press and eat it. Tastes of trousers.
9. Switch kettle on.
10. Settle down to watch *My Mother the Car* on huge black and white 1960s hotel TV.
11. Smell burning.
12. Hit top of TV with harmonica.
13. Smell burning.
14. Attempt to put burning kettle out with small plastic 1960s containers of hotel milk.
15. Run from the room shouting I TRIED TO COOK A RABBIT IN A KETTLE BUT THE KETTLE CAUGHT FIRE.
16. Realise that's a catchy tune.
17. Sing it: I TRIED TO COOK A RABBIT IN A KETTLE BUT THE KETTLE CAUGHT FIRE…

The Scream on Stockport Station

She is carrying the scream
through the darkness.

That head like a Mazda bulb
I'd know it anywhere.

She is carrying the scream
through the station.

That face like a turnip lamp from hell
I'd know it anywhere.

She is carrying the scream
past the buffet

That head like a dying balloon
I'd know it anywhere.

She's brought it home from Norway
to Stockport

to a little house in Stockport
where the person it's a portrait of

is screaming with happiness.

My Caravan's Got a Bontempi Organ in it

I drive my caravan slowly
up the A1.
I like to look at the view.

I drive my caravan very slowly
up the A1.
I like to compose songs about the view

because my caravan's got a bontempi organ in it.

I park my caravan carefully
in the field.
I like to be near the water.

I park my caravan very carefully
in the field
I like to be near the other caravanners

because my caravan's got a bontempi organ in it.

I play my bontempi organ at night
under the stars
and all the other caravanners sing along.

I play my bontempi organ all through the night
under the beautiful stars
and all the other caravanners
and sometimes, it seems,
the stars and the moon,
sing along:

> O stars like fine pimples
> on the sky's face
> o moon like a turnip
> a white one
> let the sounds of my organ
> drift into space

till the dawn
pulls skywards
the sun

because my caravan's got a bontempi organ in it.

The Ice House

Every Sunday afternoon we used to go on our Sunday afternoon
run. There were two routes. Route one: from Darfield via
Goldthorpe to Hickleton with its churchyard with the skulls in
the gate, turn left at Hickleton crossroads for a Danny's ice cream,
then past Bilham Sand quarry to Hooton Pagnell, described by
Arthur Mee in his *Counties of England* as a Jewel in a sea of coal,
then past the mysterious church in the middle of a field at Frickley
and back home. Route two: through Darfield to Millhouses,
turn left at Holly House, the old pit owner's house where the
beekeeper lived, through Middlecliffe, once called Plevna, and
Great Houghton, past Houghton Woods to a Danny's ice cream
at Brierley Crossroads. A childhood of Sundays dominated by
mysterious buildings and Danny's Ice Cream. And my dad would
always say the same things as we drove along. Past a house at the
edge of Great Houghton he'd point and say 'We now pass the
famous house of Dick Turpin, famous for his horse Black Beauty.
And now we approach the ducky pond, famous for the ducks.'

And for all those years of Sundays as we sat at Brierley
Crossroads eating ice cream, I never knew this place was here: the
ice house, deep in the woods that the man at Burntwood Hall
created for his pleasure. A treasure under the ground, melting
away.

Epic, I Mean an Epic Feel to it

What happened was that I was making the fire,
screwing up the paper, about to put the firelighters in

and one of the firelighters, a cheap firelighter,
crumbled over my trousers; soft, precise light dust

sprinkled on the black cords like stars in the night sky
over Wombwell during the dream I had on Sunday night, the one

where all the lights of Wombwell died in their sleep, except that
one. I tried to, but couldn't, force myself to sleep. Dawn

was in the dream, walking through Wombwell towards a fire
flickering just behind the Pico snack bar. I lit the fire,

brushed the firelighter from my trousers. The light.
I haven't told you which one didn't go. Which light.

It doesn't matter. I might have the same dream tonight,
the one where Wombwell is bathed in a version of night

that includes a couple of elements of day: sleeplessness,
and restlessness. Dawn suffers badly. From sleeplessness.

Grace

died, slumped
in her ice-cream van
on Wombwell market.

It's like New York City
some days at that crossroads.
I mean the traffic,

I mean the indifference.
Mr Spencer
at the Spencer Sewing Centre

hangs a tape measure
around his neck
wears it an inch longer each year

from the right
to the left. Time passes.
Like New York City,

I mean the high buildings,
I mean the indifference.
Grace knitted, slack times,

Decembers in her van.
I mean the cold,
I mean the indifference.

Mr Spencer, late December,
pulls an inch
moving closer to Grace.

Top Row/Low Row, Woolley Colliery Village

We used to say
Meet you at The Green Hut,

See you at the top
of Low Row, by the third

lamp post, him that works,
lightheaded. We used to say

I can't hear the motorway now,
you get used to her, I can't hear

the chips frying in The Green Hut
like I used to. Open every teatime.

We used to say Get off up to school,
never mind staring out of the window,

plenty of time for staring later.
We used to say

They need lights on that path,
We used to say I like the lights

on that path, we used to say
the lights on that path

are going to get broke.
Meet you at The Green Hut.

See you at the bottom
of Top Row. We used to skip

Top Row, Low Row,
Mucky washing on show.

Vests and white pants, flapping
in the wind from Russia, lightheaded.

George and Joe on a Bench: Wind-Symmetry

George, from Windhill,
hair permanently shocked
into a bush. A real bush.

Joe, Low Row,
face folded over itself,
into a slice of bread. A real slice.

On a dark night
in his garden
George could be a window.
On a dark night
in his house
Joe could be a wall.

On this bench
they could be twins.
Twin candles, twin snowmen
melting into different shapes.

That kind of twin.
That k. of t.

Brisk Coffee

I got an early train from Sheffield to Leeds the other day, then I
had to wait for a connection, so I found myself in the buffet at
7.30 a.m., clutching a steaming medium coffee and staring at my
fellow passengers. It's not that I'm nosey: I'm a writer, and that's
the kind of thing writers are supposed to do.

It was the usual buffet cross-section, I guess: men with birds
tattooed on their muscular necks, couples gazing hungrily at each
other, elderly ladies glancing incessantly from side to side, and a

few impossibly glamorous young things who must have got up at about half past three to end up looking like that at 7.30 in Leeds.

Then a man walked in, or should I say then a man walked in *briskly*. He was a brisk businessman in a brisk suit with a brisk hairdo. He did everything briskly: he strode across to the table nearest the counter and put his top-opening Briefcase down on it. He went to the counter and ordered a small coffee from the lad with lav brush hairstyle. The lad snapped a lid on the coffee and old Brisky shovelled up a few sachets of sugar. He went back to the table, prised the lid off the coffee and poured the contents of a couple of sachets of sugar into the brownish liquid. People looked at him curiously. He was more interesting to look at than the sandwiches. He stirred the coffee with a biro which he wiped briskly with a white hanky. He did not put the lid back on the coffee. He put the cup of coffee carefully into the top-opening briefcase. He snapped the briefcase shut. He strode away, swinging the briefcase jauntily.

The rest of us, the early morning buffet crowd, all stared after him then stared hard at the lid, motionless on the white formica table. He walked out of the station. He hailed a taxi by waving his briefcase in the air.

He's been haunting me ever since, that bloke. It was a momentary lapse of reason, I suppose. A little explosion in the head that makes you forget to do the things that you do so often they become instinctive, like zipping your fly up or opening the door before you walk through it. Every day he gets his coffee at 7.32. Every day he puts the lid on. But not that particular day. All week I've been speculating on why and what next?

Maybe he jumped from his taxi, sprinted into the boardroom. The boss looked up, stern as God over his half-moon glasses. 'Have you got those important documents, George?' the boss says in a voice like cracking ice. 'You mean the documents that must stay dry at all costs?' says George. 'Yes, I mean the documents that must on no account get wet,' creaks the boss. George reaches into his briefcase...

Or maybe he wasn't a businessman at all, but a spy. Maybe that quiet middle-aged woman flicking through the *People's Friend* over there by the door of the buffet was his contact. Maybe the sign to quit the safe house (you can tell I read a lot of spy novels) was the lidless coffee in the coffee-coloured briefcase. Come to think of it, she did leave soon after, leaving her *People's Friend* flapping on the table, open at a story called 'Love by the side of Loch Eck'.

Or maybe he wasn't a businessman or a spy. Maybe he was just eccentric. Maybe he'd had enough. Seize the day. No more boring old George, doing the same thing every day. The coffee in the briefcase was just the start of it. Later he'd dress up as Rasputin and startle the typing pool. Later still he'd sit in the canteen with a fake plastic hatchet in his head.

If you're reading this, George, can you let me know?

Sunset ovver Barnsley

Sithi, it were red
as red as that singlet
tha kept wearing last Summer,

as red as them tomatoes
thi fatha grew in his greenhouse
we had cartloads on em last Summer,

as red as thy face
when tha got mad wi him ont' telly
tellin kids ow ter talk,
red as a rose in Summer,

gret fat fadin sunset
blood orange
ovver Barnsley
red as the way we speyk

The Next Poem I Write

The first verse: will have the woman in it, the woman standing in the school staffroom, as the school secretary tapes a science programme from the radio. Those schools radio presenters have a certain kind of voice. The woman will be showing the school secretary her personal alarm. It would make a noise if she was attacked. The woman says, 'When you've been brayed up by a bloke it toughens you up.' The school secretary says, 'I can eat what I like and I don't get fat.'

The second verse: will have that school party in it, rushing for their bus, rushing past me as I walked round Worsbrough Res. Those white haired twins, walking at the back of the group. Two boys, alike. White hair.

The third verse: will have the butcher in it that I saw running down the road. His apron was a striped red. It will also have a question in it: why do so many butchers shops have clocks in?

Postmodernist Summer Nights in the Dearne Valley

Went to see a blues band
called the Pete Mitchell Smith
Blues Band at the Thurnscoe Hotel,
missed the last 212, walked home.

Contemplated school names
resonating like boat names
or the names of fishing flies:
Springwood, Upperwood, The Hill,

Low Valley, Sacred Heart, Lacewood.
I've got conjunctivitis. Entropy
and collapse by the Coronation Club,
turn on, attracting more, many more

than the Pete Mitchell Smith
Blues Band. Language falls in
on itself. A dead fish falling
in the bath. I know this valley

like the back of my hand. Look
at the back of my hand. It's
a mystery to me. A mystery.
Your dad's gone fishing.

On his own.

The Literary Life

This is what happened. All my family got this stomach bug, from
the baby to the four-year-old to the six-year-old to the wife.
Meanwhile, I'm in Frankfurt, representing British Poetry at a
Festival of British Writing. I get home, home is the hero, bags of
duty free gifts and little knick-knacks, and there's the family, laid
out, being sick in waste-paper bins, weeping, shaking their little
fists.

So all the duty frees go in a pile on the floor and I'm on
mopping-up duty, jet-lagged, still quivering from that little pocket
of turbulence we hit over the channel when my stomach turned
upside down and it felt like my feet were coming through my eyes.

Gradually the family get better. The duty frees and the little
knick-knacks get distributed and then of course the stomach bug
flies around the room, hits a bit of turbulence over the microwave,
and lands on me, home is the hero. The bug sits on my shoulder
and says Right, I'll get you in a minute.

This is how it happened. They're all better, I'm feeling fine. I
have to go to Wakefield to meet an Important Man in the Arts.
We meet in a Pizza Hut, that's how important he is. As I walk in,
the bug says (in a Vincent Price voice) Now is The Time, and slips
inside my stomach. I hardly notice a thing. Except I start to sweat.

And I start to yawn. My brow is like a watering can, my palms are leaking all over the menu. The Important Man in the Arts notices this. He says, 'Are you feeling okay?' and I say 'Is it warm in here or is it just me?' Then he says something very profound and important and I yawn a great big Jaw Cracker. I think maybe it's hunger pangs so I start to eat the pizza and the bug unpacks its suitcases and starts to hang its family portraits on my stomach wall.

I have a pudding. By this time my face is like Victoria Falls and I can hardly keep awake. Whatever the Important Man in the Arts says I just nod at. Very slowly. The bug plays football in my stomach, then it plays rugby, then lacrosse, then cricket then basketball. We leave the Pizza Hut. I'm staggering like a man who's had 15 pints. It's like turbulence: my feet feel like they're about to come through my eyes.

Somehow I get home. Home is the hero, looking like a man who's been swimming with his clothes on. During the meal my biro burst in my pocket, so I've got Dadaist patterns all over my shirt. I think that I can defeat the bug by sheer willpower. I loll in agony on the settee, summoning up willpower. The bug laughs its head off in my stomach.

Unpleasant things happen in the bathroom. I won't go into them. The sun glints on the sink, the children's toys have an innocent air, certain sounds can be heard. I summon up willpower, it doesn't work. I feel like a child of three.

I go to bed, can't be bothered to shut the curtains, can't be bothered to get undressed, leave me alone, ink from the burst biro all over my shirt, socks itching.

Suddenly it's the middle of the night. I'm hot. The bed appears to be full of rubble. The baby is in bed with us, snoring loudly. He sounds like a JCB. I toss and turn, turn and toss. Find that I feel slightly better if I lay on my back and lift up my left leg. It seems to help. The bug attacks me with a lump hammer. I get out of bed, sweating like a melting snowman. Downstairs its cool. Nice and cool. I sit on the settee, just for a minute. I'll be all right in a minute. Leave me alone. Print all over one side of my head. I fall asleep, have two dreams.

First dream: I'm at the side of the road. It's misty. A strange glass ambulance comes past. It's full of brides and grooms looking out, waxy. Second dream: I hail a taxi. It stops. I give the driver a teapot. 'Can you take this to my house?' I say.

I wake up. Where am I? On the settee. Rough cushion, my face all creased. Creased on one side, print on the other. My wife comes in. It's morning. 'You've got a column to write,' she says. This is what happened.

The Continuity Girl has Died

Came in through the door
in a red hat, came through
the door in a blue hat,
stick in the right hand,

the left hand, the one
with the ring, the one
without the ring, the sense
of loss obvious in the

breaking face, the smile
lighting the room, the tears
cascading like bath water,
the grin big banana under

the blue hat, black hat,
red hat, no hat, stick
in this hand or that hand,
the socks plain, patterned,

the chin bristling, the chin
smooth, shaved, unshaved,
gleaming under the blue hat,
red hat, stick, no stick,

tears, smile, ring, no ring.

Great Dogs of History

Rin Tin Tin, of course, and Lassie,
and the nameless dogs, the ones
at the edge of paintings, at the edge

of a child's mind before it goes to sleep,
at the edge of a child's painting
on the fridge door. The dog that howled

and woke Jesus up in his manger
but he never cried and just looked,
smiling, at the gifts the men brought,

the men at the edge of the picture.
The faithful dog who waited for years
beside his master's grave, because

his master said he had gone for food
and the master is always right
listen to his voice, at the edge

of the fridge. The dog who brought
news of the deaths of all those
people, all those people

and he never cried and just looked,
and this dog and that dog and
the paw prints at the edge of the fridge

and this dog. Woof. This dog. Bark.
Oh, Lassie of course, and Rin Tin Tin,
barking. The men at the edge of the picture.

The Veins in my Neck

Sunset in Howell Wood;
midwinter sunset
like a fire going out.

The veins in my neck
stand out like drainpipes
when I'm angry.

Look at my dad in this photo
holding a fish
as big as himself.

It's a life, this.
Look at it. It's
a life in sunsets,

sunsets and fish.
Midwinter sunsets
like fires going out.

Black against red,
headgear and sky.
If it was a sound

it would be the sound
a burning tree makes
in heavy rain.

Migrations and exiles,
pithead to pithead,
Ayrshire to Yorkshire

like fires going out;
sunset, smoke,
midwinter drainpipes

as big as himself.
Lots of men in this wood
walking babies and children.

Midwinter sunset,
time on your hands
like a fish

as big as yourself,
a fire going out,
a life in sunsets.

Beethoven was Deaf, You Know

Recently there have been
two car chases round Darfield
in the early early hours.

During one car chase
I was pissing in a bus shelter
and I didn't hear the car chase
but they heard me pissing.

Car chase.

Car
chase.

You stand the words on top of each other.
Make a little tower.
Such a modern thing, a car chase.

Fact: Shakespeare could not have written about a

car
chase.

It's too modern.

But a car chase
that you can't hear.
How modern is that?

'Many of McMillan's poems
take place at night'
Because most of your life
takes place at night.

Here, chase this.
It's only a toy
but it works.
Wind it up.
Make a little tower
Such a modern thing, a machine,

a poem, a car
chase.

In a West Yorkshire Bus Queue, Several Mature Art Students Discuss Excitedly the Earthquake of April 2nd 1990

I was leaning against the wall,
phoning my husband/a present from
Polperro, it just fell to the ground,
drifted like a leaf. The light
in St Ives/he works in Oldham and he said

Yes, Yes, I can feel it too!

I was in my studio, well I call it/
I ran out onto the lawn to stand,
to experience it and well, my dear,
I had quite forgotten, quite forgotten

that I was naked!

my studio, it's really the shed.
The paints ran, I swear the paints
ran down the canvas/at first

I covered my breasts!

I'm working on a new piece,
two people, leaning against walls,
miles apart!

November 1963 in a Scotland of the Mind

The milkman is framed
in the glass door.

John Kennedy is dressing
to be shot

again and again
in films for ever,

later. The milkman
is holding

a Scottish pound note
for my dad

the village's one
Scotsman.

Jock, they call him.
It isn't his name.

Upstairs, he is dressing,
pulling on his trousers

singing an Andy Stewart
song, probably

Donald Where's Yer Troosers,
I think.

The Making of the English Working Class

George dreams of silence.
Isobel sleeps in the wash house.
Olive weeps in hedges.

Alice sprains her wrist polishing.
Harry writes to his wife.
Charlie drives someone's car into town.

Arthur can't hear what you say.
Doris can't find her finger.
Henry is laughed at.

Sammy feels his neck breaking.
Danny falls overboard.
Jacky stares at nothing.

Tommy sees his arm in the machine.
Jimmy walks to Rochdale.
Nelly coughs in her room.

Eddie can't move.
Barry vomits into a scarf.
Annie looks up at the roof fall.

Billy has lost the use of his legs.
Sally has scars an inch deep.
Willy dribbles down his cardigan.

From

I Found This Shirt

(1998)

I'd Better Not

A man leaned over to a man
In a pub and said, in a voice,
'I used to be 37
But now I'm 51'

And that's how the years go,
In handfuls, like somebody
Is almost at the end
Of a bag of crisps

And they tip the bag up
And it's as though they're
Drinking crisps. That's
How the years go.

Today, one of my daughters
Is 13, and one of my daughters
Is 11. My son is 8. I'm 40.
My wife is 41. My dad is 77.

My mam is 74. That is how
The years go. Very bleached,
Is the grass on that coast;
I was going to explain that,

Fill you in. I just had to
Answer the phone and somebody
Asked me if I was a photographer.
Once, one of my daughters

Was 1, one of my daughters
Wasn't born, my son wasn't
Born, I was 28, my wife was
29, my dad was 65,

My mam was 62, and I took
A photograph. Very bleached,
Is the grass on that coast.
That is how the years go.

My Dog

April is the Cruellest Month
might seem like a strange name for a dog,
and sometimes I think it is
when I'm shouting her name
on the high moors
in the driving wind.

'April is the Cruellest Month!'
I shout,
'April is the Cruellest Month'
and my dog runs up to me,
barking, wagging her tail,
and I feel slightly, ever so slightly
embarrassed.

But then when people say
as they walk by me
on the high moors
in the driving wind,
'Can a month bark?'
'Can April wag its tail?'
I swell with pride
because my dog's name
is image, and metaphor, and poetry.

So,
'April is the Cruellest Month'
I shout, and
'April is the Cruellest Month'
and the words roll round my mouth
like Easter Eggs in a Shopping Basket
which is the name of my cat.

Self Portrait

Face a red planet
smudged by glasses, he's
slumped in the bus seat

As the sun rises, illuminating
the little bits of whisker
he's missed, iron filings

On the nodding red planet.
How small his hands are.
How Elvis his hair is.

He may be a collapsing balloon,
chins folded like dough,
sun reflects on the glasses.

Tuesdays and Wednesdays

I imagined it would be a sad place
The last room before death

A place of tears and silence
A slow dwindling to the last breath.

It isn't: it's a place of affirmation
That *now* is important, not the hereafter

It taught me a lot: how to listen,
How to take each story as fresh and new,

How we can all teach each other a lesson
How the telling of a life makes a life true:

And it confirmed what I'd suspected all along
That everyone's artistic in a personal way

Art's what makes us human and our song
Sings from the morning to the close of the day.

Home Support

It is mid-July, 1997. It is hot.
Barnsley are in the Premier League,
and in my head our season
is laid out as simple as an Underground Map,
or a child's drawing of the solar system.
Mid-July, a pre-season friendly
against Doncaster. The start of something
and one of my daughters is coming to Doncaster
on her own for the first time on the bus
to meet me to go to the match. As the bus
rolls into the bus station I see her red shirt
upstairs, and she waves, and my heart breaks

for her, and me, and her red shirt with 21 TINKLER
on the back, and the bus driver who is a Middlesbrough fan,
and the other people who tumble off the bus in their red shirts
with the season laid out in their heads simple and lovely
as a map of the solar system or a child's drawing
of the Underground, and the Greek bus station toilet attendant
who knows me and shouts PREMIER LEAGUE, but
mostly it breaks for her, and me, and her red shirt.

Still, it's July. It's hot. We meet Chris and Duncan
and we try to go into a pub even though my daughter's
a bit young and a man in a suit says Sorry, Home Support Only.
And my heart breaks

for her, and me, and her red shirt, and the Home Support
who cheer Doncaster and whose season is laid out simple
as a serving suggestion, or a child's drawing of a football team,
but mostly it breaks for her and me.

We get a taxi home, which seems extravagant, but I think
of the Greek toilet attendant and I shout PREMIER LEAGUE
on our path as we walk into the house, father and daughter, red
shirt, hot night, Home Support, season laid out in our heads
simple and lovely as a football programme, simple and lovely
as a penalty kick, a well-taken corner.

Poem Containing Several R.E.M. Song Titles

It's a hot Summer's evening.
My wife flicks a moth out of the door
With her bra. It could have been my

Shirt, or the *Radio Times*. The sun
Has got his hat on, and the garden's
Almost dark. The hedgehog'll

Be out soon. The big wheel is going
Round, says my wife in a different place
And a different time. I'd like

To help with the moth, but I'm all
Tangled up with some fishing line
That my son left under the ironing

Board, so I'm like a swan, tangled
In the invisible knots that can choke
You or at least stop you flying.

from *I Found This Shirt*   123

There's a storm somewhere in the air
Which is the best place for it. It's hard
To be a moth, or a swan, or a hedgehog,

Or a big wheel. Spot them all.

Endless Shedness

lift lid of shed peer into
endless shedness below

a kind of blue sky shedness
a kind of endless shedness
like the corners you find in sheds

like your shed has more corners
than you thought possible

endless shedness
you always find things in your shed
that you never put there
that your parents never put there
that your children never put there
endless shedness

try this now
with your own shed
and you will find the
(endless shedness)
things that were never put there

```
endless shedness
endless shed
e    ess s      ess
e    e    e    e
      less shed
      less  hed
cndless shed
endless shed
```

Poem Is a City

Poem is a city. Dark corners.
You sleep under blankets
in a poem. In the shop doorway,

in the underpass of a poem.
It is as though you cannot live
anywhere else except in a poem

is a city. Under blankets. Dark
blankets. From a moving train
you see into the houses,

the landscape is a windowscape,
a kitchenscape. 'Ah,' you say,
poetically, 'what a delightful

kettlescape in that kitchen'
because poem is a city, city
is a poem. Underpass of a poem.

Happiness on the First Train
from Barnsley to Huddersfield

The happiness creeps up on you,
in the dark train as we stop at Dodworth,

then Silkstone Common, then Penistone,
and some people are sleeping and sleeping

is a sort of happiness, and those three men
who are always on this train are talking

and talking is a form of happiness, and I
am looking, and looking is a kind of

happiness. Then the train pulls out
of Penistone Station, across that impossibly

beautiful viaduct that I can never
remember the name of, and the light

is arriving in the sky as if by slow train,
and now I can remember the name

of the viaduct and the name
of the viaduct is Happiness,

Happiness high across the slowly
lightening fields.

Free Improvising Musician Drops Frying Pan

Crash of it so random, depends
on all sorts: type of floor. Type
of frying pan. Position of the bacon and the eggs.

I'll incorporate it into the gig tonight,
somehow. Filtered through the day, of course,
the things I haven't done yet,

sounds I've not heard. Tonight's music
starts now, nice and early, this morning,
frying pan in mid air really the start of it,

start of all improvisation, the music
not yet heard, the bacon not yet

in a pattern on the floor, the eggs
running, running to keep up

with themselves. Keeping up with itself:
the music not yet played, not yet heard.

From
Perfect Catch

(2000)

Malvern Link, Early Morning

'You just walk across the green' they said
and here I am, walking across the green,

as the sun lights up my smeared glasses
and I look like a kind of Owl: the Fat

Anoraked Owl, walking to the first train
as the sun lights up the smeared sky

and I walk across the green,
just like they said, across the green.

Branwell Brontë is Reincarnated as a Vest

I hang here like a ghost
on the midnight line

frost hardens me, hardens the frocks
I hang with.

Irony to hang here on
a night crashing with the loud moon,

the moon only I can hear.

I hang here like a ghost
on the midnight line;

If you stand by the garden shed,
there, that side of the garden shed

and look at me from that angle,
look towards the washing line from that angle,

I'm almost invisible behind the frocks.

I hang here like a ghost.
The frost hardens
and dawn is dark years away.

Lumb Bank, 1978

In the kitchen: me,
Charles Sisson, David Wright,
the ex-mayor of Shaftesbury

and a man who was so nervous
that he had to shout his poems
from another room

so that nobody could see him.
David Wright held one of my poems
in the steam.

Something starts here.

A House of Bricks

Oh, it's that old game,
the making-up-the-collective-noun
game. I'm good at that.

They come to me as easy as fish
come to the shop in a van
from Grimsby. A field

of crop circles. A van of fish.
That's the kind of thing.
Collective nouns are easy.

A hairnet of hair.
A sunset of clouds.
A case of matching luggage.

It's easy this. Goodnight.
Keep in touch. A keep in touch
of friends. A calendar of months.

A fiery hell. Maybe not quite,
that one. Maybe not.
Language is so easy, so

easy. Goodnight all.
Keep in touch.

Body and Bone: The Fat Man in the Bath

Feels like I've been in this bath
for a thousand years, wrinkled
from the toenail to the hair's tip
like the paper in this magazine.

Feels like I've been in this bath
for a thousand long wet years
as history wrinkles around me
like my thumb in this water.

Feels like I've been in this bath
for ever, drawing my smiley face
in the steam on the window
like a cave painting of a fat man:

The Long Man of Barnsley.
Well, the short man. The mouth
open, singing a wordless song,
my mouth a big O.

Been in this bath a thousand years;
feels like the centre of life, here
and now, me singing, me wrinkled.
I'm a body, a bone, a wrinkle

and something more. My kids
are banging on the bathroom door
saying Let Us In, Let Us In.
Kate, Lizzie, Andrew, the world is yours;

have it, play with it, roll it like a football
is rolled just before a free kick. The world
might be wrinkled, might be steamed up,
but it's yours to play with

for at least a thousand years.
Kate, Lizzie, Andrew, we're body and bone,
bone and body, but so much more,
so much more. Draw in the steam,

write in the steam, before it fades.
Feels like I've been in this bath
for a thousand years, a thousand
long, wet, wrinkled years.

Slip of a Man

These tiny poems were written as a collaborative work with the painter Richard Barnes. I've always written fairly long pieces, and I'm enjoying the chance of making really short works.

I Rested

The bricks of hotel butter against
the kettle in which I could
see my face.

Slip of a Man

A man standing on the slippery roof of the Holiday Inn
in Chesterfield. Careful, mate!

Numbers Game

of the 23 people in this carriage
6 look dangerous
11 are staring at my egg

From a Train Window

steam trees (imagine
it as a photograph).

Written on a Train Window

in dust: 11.30
train is a moving dust clock
and time has stopped

My Co

ffee smells li
  ke fi
    sh

Truths

People are lying on their mobile phones.
I'm on an aeroplane.
I'm on a dog.
I'm on a cloud.
I'm on a long, long beach of mud.

Everything replying to everything else.

Going

'I love you both'
in dust on the train window.

My glasses
fall onto a newspaper,

now the child in the photograph
is wearing my glasses.

Taxi

'Took two women
all the way to London.
They got out,
stood in Oxford Street
for half an hour,
not moving,
then I brought them home.
Four hundred
quid.'

Barnsley's

Unique magnetic coastal railway.

Colours

On my walk through the cemetery
I am almost part of a funeral.

All in black, apart from
a man in a yellow anorak.

A boy turns, punches away tears,
gently.

Dream

Mr Lowe next door
on a high ladder,

pointing to an aeroplane.
I say

'On those steps
you're closer to the sky.'

Journey

The man on the train says
'I literally
started the book this morning.'
Somewhere, angels are laughing.

Gas Fire

There was no bowling, they
simply sat, the fronts
of their faces very
hot from the gas fire.

Meter

At 6 am in Cumwhitton
the only lights
are the stars, the moon,
the taxi's lights, the taxi's meter,
the numbers on my mobile phone,
the lights in the house I've just left,
the light in the house opposite,
the winking aeroplane, the staring cat.

Obsessive

We are talking
on a perfect morning.

'I walked down the line
from Carlisle to the goods yard,
no coloured vest, no hat, no flag,
only me and the others
walking down the line.'

Sour

Just my Dad's face
as he eats the orange,
the eye rolling
to the back, the very back
of his head.

Thursday

The briefcase hung in the night air,
then dropped into the dark waters of the Ouse.

I Took Him

Four tangerines in a bag. He
was asleep, but one of the men
in his ward looked dead, eyes rolled
upwards.

Morning

The woman next door in her nightie
is dropping bread on the lawn
and the bread, or the woman, or the nightie,
activates the security light.

Tickets

I bought tickets for the wrestling
and they were strange tickets; they were
pink slips with the word WRESTLING on them

so on your train you would have a pink slip
with JOURNEY

in the café a pink slip with FOOD.

from *Perfect Catch*　139

Moon and Rabbit

The moon preceded the bus
all the way to Doncaster.
    The rabbit couldn't stand up,
looked at me with an eye like a marble
that a child had made from cardboard.
Hutch. Bus. Moon. A kind of
triangle. On the train, a woman
tears a shape of paper from *The Star*
to use as a bookmark in a book
she hasn't started yet.

Instead

Instead of combing my hair
I get it cut.
Instead of washing it. Cut.

Before he cuts it the barber says
You should comb it. Wash it, maybe.

He combs it,
pretends to cut.

Aviary

birds eye walls
walls eye birds
eye birds walls
eye walls birds

Visit

In the lounge of Ward 4
at Mount Vernon hospital
he is talking to his mother
but he is looking
at a single walnut
under her chair.

Dennis's First Story which tells us something about friendship

Giving the man the whisky
and he asked
Are you a morris dancer?

Dennis's Second Story which tells us something about age

The pound note blowing under the bank gates.
The fishing net.
The young man leaping over the gates.

Pieces

of
broken soap.

My Life

I said to my wife
'I'll keep my magazines
in the cupboard.'

On the Train, by the Sea

The blind man
said to his wife
'This is where
we came motorcycling.'

Café, Totnes

The taxi driver tips
all the pepper from the pot
onto his scrambled egg.
It's a tower.
It's a film.

Career

At last he found time
to write a novel
but wasted it
sitting in the fridge
looking at the cheese.

Taunton

A vicar in a leather trilby!

My

Pocket map

That Man

reading yesterday's paper
is disorientating me.

The Mexico Poems

In September 1997 I was invited to Mexico by The British Council. I made some programmes for Yorkshire Television while I was there, with my mate the producer/director Dave Beresford. Dave's also an artist, and when we came back we put together an exhibition of six poems and six paintings. The exhibition went to Mexico in June 2000, and Dave did six more paintings and I did six more poems; I've tried to link Mexico and Barnsley, since Barnsley is the filter I see everything through.

She Watched him Approaching with the Rose in Oaxaca

Earlier that afternoon, the band had played, and when
she thought about it later, it was as though the band
had been playing underwater, the notes were so distant,
so distorted, soaking wet, and now as he came closer she
could still hear the band, playing very close to her ear,
playing music that became the white vest and the rose,
playing music that became the look on his face, playing
as though they were all underwater.

He Gave Her a Rose in Oaxaca

In the decades to come
all you will remember
are the key images from that night;

the guitars, the bottles,
the light from the square,
the spoons, the basket of roses

and the rose. The song stopped
as if shot. The man gave her a rose.
He was wearing a white vest.

Her face turned red. In the decades
not yet arrived, the night will become
a jumble of colours: the brown light

of the guitar, the white light
of the vest, the rose's light.
And in many, many years

maybe it will just be a rose
or a memory of a rose,
which is not quite the same thing.

Flat Bull

Excess baggage, they wanted to call it,
but I insisted it was hand luggage.

They compromised: it sat next to me
on the plane back to England, the flat bull.

At home, I kept it in the garden,
where it wandered about, flatly.

Sometimes you could see it,
sometimes it was just a line against the trees.

Mr Lowe next door
was doing his garden;

'What's that?' he said,
his flat cap just above the hedge.

'It's a flat bull,' I said:
'I brought it back from Mexico.'

That night he tried to fight it,
rushing at it with his fork,

losing his flat cap,
breaking his glasses,

shouting and grunting,
his wife watching from the window,

doing the ironing.

A Plastic Garden from the Window of the Hotel Bristol, Mexico City

Dave was asleep, and I was watching *The Fugitive*
on the hotel TV, and I heard the children playing

in the school opposite the hotel, and I went to open
the window, and I looked down to their yard

which wasn't a yard, it was a garden with plastic grass,
and plastic flowers, and the children sat in the corner

of the plastic in their uniforms and waited for their parents.
On the TV Harrison Ford and Tommy Lee Jones exchanged

shouts which started from their brains in English, but
were dubbed into Spanish on the way to their mouths,

and I wondered if the children heard the shouts on their
green plastic, wondered if they heard somebody being

accused of something they didn't do, in a language which
wasn't the one he was born with. The plastic grass was

green, so green. The flowers were so colourful.
The children were so young. Harrison Ford.

Skull made of chocolate
Skull made of sky
Skull made of edible earth
Skull made of memories
Skull held in the hand
Skull made of chocolate
Skull of Uncle Charlie
Skull made of singing
Skull crushed by roof falling
Skull that floated
Skull made of chocolate
Skull that sank
Skull of the tiniest bird
Skull of Mr. Page
Skull of the day before
Skull made of chocolate
Skull of tomorrow
Skull of today's date
Skull of today
Skull shopping
Skull made of chocolate
Skull of Grandma Fullilove
Skull held in the sky
Skull of next year
Skull of first sod cut for the new pit
Skull made of chocolate
Skull of the night
Skull of the Beano
Skull of the Fish and Chip shop
Skull of Cousin Ron
Skull made of chocolate
Skull of the bloody head
Skull of the headscarf
Skull of the flat cap
Skull of the balaclava
Skull made of chocolate
Skull water

Skull moon
Skull moon's reflection in
Skull water
Skull made of chocolate
Skull rippling reflection in
Skull lake
Skull boat
Skull of Uncle Jack
Skull fishing

Day of the Dead

This day. This day
above all others
would be a good day to die,

as the chocolate skulls
begin to melt
in the not-so-fierce

sun of evening,
and the parades grow noisier
and the singing

becomes less like singing
and more like dancing,
this would be a good day to die,

a good day to vacate your skull
your skull that melts with memories.

1

From one side: flat bull.
From one side: flat bull.
From ahead: almost no bull at all.
From behind: almost no flat bull at all.

2

This bull comes to me in nightmares
This bull comes to me in dreams
This bull could slip under your bedroom door
This bull isn't all that he seems

3

The bull
in a bullooon
fell too soon
from the moon

4

Flat bull on a hill
fall and flattened the bullfighter
flat bullfighter
flat bullfighter's mother ran to help
flat bull on a hill
fell and flattened the flat bullfighter's mother
flat flat bullfighter's mother
flat bullfighter's father ran to help
flat bull on a hill
fell and flattened the flat bullfighter's father
flat flat bullfighter's father

5

Flat bull on a hill
Flat bull
Flat   on a hill
Flat   ull
F at bull

```
F     ull
F           ill
F           ill
F at bull on a hill
F   u       ll
F   u       ll
F at bull on a hill
Flat        hill
```

A Plastic Garden

From the air, Mexico City ends abruptly,
a line drawn down a page
between city and not-city.
In the years since my visit
one image has nudged me
in the ribs almost daily:
that plastic garden, those children
playing in that plastic garden,
that grass, greener than any grass,
those children, more real
than any children. In one sense
it's an image that's almost too perfect
for a poet, a loaded image, an image
that, if you leave it alone, will sing
and move along the ground as if propelled
by a little motor. I prefer not to think
of it as a poet would, though, but rather
as a city would, or as a line
between city and not-city.

Descending into Chihuahua, Descending into Barnsley

On the X19, as we slow into Barnsley Bus Station,
the lights of the Gala Bingo sing their impossible dreams,

the lights of Oakwell dance their impossible dreams,
and the light of a young girl
lighting a cigarette
as she waits for her boyfriend
to come out of the paper shop
light up her face for an instant
as the lights of the bus rake across the bus station
as though the bus station
is being photocopied.

All descents
into lights
are impossibly beautiful.

Descending into Chihuahua

other journeys, ferry rolling into Coll, meeting a man who guessed
where I came from in three guesses, to the exact village, to the
hospital with my Dad late on a Saturday night, I'm afraid you've
suffered a slight stroke Mr McMillan and then home in a taxi and
as I climb out an aeroplane is crossing the black to somewhere,
I can see the lights, he was sitting in this pub on the Isle of Coll
covered in soot because he'd been sweeping chimneys and he
guessed, he guessed exactly where I came from

the lights of the airstrip   the mountains

other journeys, bus pausing in Phoenix and a man telling about
how they were burning his city block by block and in three
months, he calculated three months, they'd be at his house, of
course there were aeroplanes overhead, of course, that man on the
Isle of Coll, later, in the graveyard cutting the grass he was too
drunk to talk, didn't even remember who I was

the mountains   the lights of the airstrip

other journeys, pushing the buggy down to the nursery and I
slipped in the park in the ice and fell down in the snow and
overheard there was an aeroplane and I bounced, really bounced
my back for a moment I didn't know where, picked up hitching by
a man called Adrian took me all the way from Barnsley to London
didn't speak until we were nearly there then he said I don't drink
beer I wallow in it and that's me used to be a hairdresser and it's
who people are different to who you think they are

the airstrip   The lights of the mountains

other journeys, all other journeys, melted down into the gold of
                                                       this one
other journeys, all other journeys, melted down into the gold of
                                                       this one

The Skinned Man

> All I am is my scream,
> no skin to speak of, to
> talk about; my scream
> is the skinless one. All
>
> I am is my scream, but
> the word scream is too harsh
> for history so I will replace it
> with the word piano.
>
> All I am is my piano.
> My blood wrenching piano;
> they stripped away
> all my skin, and left me

a piano. Look carefully;
you can just about
see the eyes. Listen:
piano, piano, piano.

The Skinned Man: a child's counting game for performer and audience

How many skins have I got?
  Too many!
  Just the one!
How many skins do I need?
  Too many!
  Just the one!
Peel off one, what do you get?
  Too many!
  Just the one!
Peel off ten, what do you get?
  Too many!
  Just the one!
Peel off a hundred, what do you get?
  Too many!
  Just the one!
Peel off them all, what do you get?
  Too many!
  Just the one!
See him running down the burning street!
  Too many!
  Just the one!
Skinless hands and skinless feet!
  Too many!
  Just the one!
He's the most skinned man you could hope to meet!
  Too many!
  Just the one!

This Lake Used to Be Frozen: Lamps
(2011)

It's Only a Novelty Coronation Street Alarm Clock

Put it in with the ham, then.
Shall we get some nails
For you to hang it up, crucify
It like Christ?

And then in the evening
We'll take it down
And put it in a cupboard.
And we'll eat the ham.

At the weekend, it will rise
Out of the cupboard,
Hang itself back up on the wall.
A miracle, I call it,

Like Martha Longhurst
Back from the snug with wings.

Tom Jones

Chorus:
My right hand leg,
My left hand foot

The old town looks
The same as I
Step down from the
Train. I was refereeing
A rugby match in Grimethorpe

Chorus:
My right hand leg
My left hand foot

And a kid on a motorbike
Came across the pitch
Right across the pitch, and
There to meet
Me is my momma

Chorus:
My right hand leg
My left hand foot

And poppa, sacks of coal
Tied to the back
Of the bloody
Bike and do you
Know what I did?

Chorus:
My right hand leg
My left hand foot

I blew the bloody whistle!

Chorus:
My right hand leg
My left hand foot

Two lines placed at the end:
The man is drawing a heart in pencil.
The colonel's sidecar.

A Miniature

I hovered outside the door
Waiting for news of the conflict.
Someone had written the number 16
On the door even though I knew
It was number 56. How war
Changes things, makes them more numerical
Somehow. My gun was heavy in my hands
Which made the hovering more difficult. The news,
When it came, was purple, with tinges of mahogany
And the insistent sound of a triangle. Military music,
As Mr. Krebs said in the pool of light.

It's the 4th of July!

Always, for me, the struggle
Between populism and
Linguistically interesting work

But, in the taxi, Roy
Is talking about Radio Sheffield
And our John is talking about

His recent holiday
On the Isle of Skye
Like this

BUT I'VE HEARDJust one nightTHEY'RE GOING TO
COMBINE ALL THE PROGRAMMESwe got the midges,
one walkWELL NEARLY ALL AND JUSTcovered, our
faces coveredJUST KEEP BREAKFAST AND TEATIME

And that's hard to represent, poetry lovers.
Later, on Doncaster station, our John tells me about the bridge
that links Skye to the mainland. He points across to Platform 4,
where a trainspotter is writing something down in his notebook.
It was only from here to there. We had a nice meal in a café.
What was it called? (That's me, asking. I've got an espresso in my
hand.)
The café.

At this point, at ten to six in the morning,
I have no idea that fourteen hours later
I will cough violently and my wife will say
'that echoed off the piano!'

Sleeper

Just before we went into the cinema
To watch Woody Allen's film,
And this is how pretentious I was as a young man,
I said to my girlfriend who has been my wife
For many years 'not all the people in the room
Will get all the jokes but you will
And I will.' Ten minutes in, we saw
A torchlight at the edge of the screen, two
Policemen came in from behind the screen
They shone torches in our faces. 'There's
Been a bomb scare' one of them said.
And we had to leave for a while
And then go back in. Let's face it,
My beard looked ridiculous. I thought
It made me look clever[1]. I think
The way my bearrrrrd unrrrrrravelled
Was parrrrrrt of my unease when
We went back in. And I found I was
Motorrrrrrbiking my rrrrrrrs!

We rrrran forrrrr the last bus.
My bearrrrrrrd continued to
Unrrrrrrrrrrrrrrrrrrrrrrrrrrrrrrravel.
The last bus of the day, of courrrrrse,
Not the last bus everrrrrrrrrrrrrr.
In my memorrrrry it was rrrrraining
But that is just because it is rrrrrrraining
As I wrrrrrrrrrrite this. Ah, my
Unrrrrrrrrrrrrrrrrrrrrrrrrravelling bearrrrrrrd!
On the bus I made a verrbal joke
About sex to coverrrr my unease.²

1 When I was at junior school I knew all the names of the moons of Jupiter.
   All of them. Every single one. So I didn't need a beard.
2 Not tonight, dearrr, I've got a head.

Old Age

Old age
Is simply this:
Put a pinny on
To do the pots
Then forget
And put
Another pinny
On to do the
Pots. Pinny on
Pinny. Two-pinny
Morning. PinnyPinny
Fastened at the back.
A pinny on a pinny.
A double pinny moment.
And the pots not
Done.

Norman Stopped Me on the Street

Norman stopped me on the street
And he said
Hey, Ian lad

Ah cud gu t't theatre
If ah wanted, ah reckon.

Ah cud sit theer an clap
At end an shart moor

An then ad gu om and seh
Wheer hev yore bin?

T't shop? T't bus stop?
T't wall? T't shed?

Ah bin t't theatre.
Av gorra programme.

Ah cud du that Ian.
Nowt stopping mi, is there?

Not a Real Bear, But a Bear Nevertheless

a play called A Winter's Tale *would immediately indicate to contemporary audiences that the play would attempt an 'idle tale', an old wives' tale not intended to be realistic and offering the prospect of a happy ending.* Wikipedia(!)

it is not known whether Shakespeare used a real bear or an actor in a bear costume Wikipedia(!)

The real bear died, writhing. Couldn't stand
The rackety trip from the bear pit, heart broke,
Blood blobbing from the mouth, a low moan

That was just this gasping side of a growl,
Just the head-wind and motley side of a growl.
So they flung-chucked its heavy furry shape

Into the soupy river and told me, sharp-like,
To get in my bear-costume and stand ready.
I've got to pursue someone apparently, as they exit.

Hm. Is history always going to be like this,
I wonder? The stand-in standing in for the real,
Dead, thing? My wife says I should have been

A philosopher. Maybe I'll see Mr. Shakespeare,
They say he gazes and scribbles and crosses out
Even as the play's on. I'll shout to him, from inside

My bear head: 'Will the stand in always stand-in
For the real, dead thing? Will the real, dead, thing
Float down the river while the stand-in spouts his line?

Is that what art is, Mr. S?' Of course he won't be able
To hear me, I'll be muffled by the bear head. The head always
Muffles art, of course, as the head muffles the heart. Ah!

I made a play with language, like The bonny Bard does. Even
Those of us with our voices strangled by our heads
Can make play with words. Nobody hears us, more's the pity.

I'm on in a moment. I've got to pursue a fellow. But
I look up just before I jam the bear's head on my bare head
(Playing again!) and I see the real bear, a bear-island,

Floating down towards the sea. The real sea. The sea.

Walk

0. *Walk from Many Points of View, Some Diverging, Some Obscured by Rain*

He's there again, that Ian McMillan, walking down the hill,
scribbling in a notebook, sometimes looking up or down
or across. Sometimes he stops and once I saw him gaze

upwards at the moon or a passing cloud. I pass him
on my bicycle and we nod. I can hardly see him,
myself. The rain's made my glasses fogbound. I can hear

a cockerel and a fast car. I'm the ghost of somebody
who once stood in a queue at the National Provincial Bank
at the bottom of Snape Hill and Ian McMillan walks through me

every morning. It tickles. Rain. Car. Cockerel. Bicycle.
A form of puzzle, if you can get that idea. A puzzle.

1. *Walk 1*

Top Field to Bottom Club, Snape Hill down past the Dancing School,
Route I took as a child to the Valley, once dropped a threepenny bit
In the postbox by the butcher's gone now, postbox gone now,

Threepenny bit in a postman's pocket or left in the box,
I like to think it was left in the box, sealed in the box when the box
Was sealed. Bottom Club to Top Field in the mist one afternoon

In the mid-1960s. Turned at the top of the hill, looked down
Into The Valley and saw the headgear of Darfield Main pointing
Through the murk. 'That's Blackpool Tower' a kid said, a big kid,

Maybe a kid from the big school. I said it wasn't and he put his face
So close to me it hurt. 'It's Blackpool Tower. You can see Blackpool
From here. You can see Blackpool from Darfield. You can see

Blackpool from Darfield.' He repeated certain words a lot. Darfield.
Blackpool. I used to call for Sheryl Lang and we'd walk
Down to the Valley and one day a dog stood watching us. Eyes. Fur.

We hid. We hid in the trees on the Inkerman fields. Bushes, trees.
The dog was a long way away but it still looked like a dog. Fur.
Eyes. After an hour we walked home, walked into our house's

Unfamiliar mid-morning light. 'Did it bark?' my mother asked.
'It just looked at us.' I said. Sheryl agreed. That threepenny bit,
Sealed up. That dog with the eyes and the fur. Blackpool Tower.

2. *A Walk Where Almost Nothing Happened*

Set off. Steps; listen, you can hear my steps. Top
Of Darfield, and then the descent down Snape Hill
And some days I feel the history and I can smell

The past but today there is nothing. Grey sky and
Then more grey. A grey cloud obscures the sun. Look:
No, sorry, nothing. Can you walk the same walk for

Decades and (steps, listen you can hear my steps on
The road) suddenly get nothing out of it. Maybe. Today.
Nothing. Grey tinge to the grey grey. Until: that donkey

Looking at the sky, that plastic bag held in that wire,
That bird singing fit to bust on that roof…

Phew. Made it to somewhere.

3. *Crying*

If you went to the old library down Snape Hill and it was sunny
You could get the librarian to stand by the old RINGTON'S TEA
Sign on the window and the words RINGTON'S TEA would appear

Back to front on her head. Like a tattoo, eh? She once passed me
A Henry Rider Haggard book with the words: I think
You're ready for this. In February 1964 I was walking up

From Low Valley with my Auntie after school. We went up the
Inkerman Road fields and there was old mucky snow
On the ground. I kicked a lump and I didn't realise there was a

Brick underneath it. I broke my leg. My Auntie had to carry me
Home on her back like I was a parcel. Later, the doctor said
'He's smashed a greenstick' and I cried. In the fog I once

Lost my Auntie and Sheryl Lang as we walked home from school.
They faded into the fog like they were sitting in a cloud. 'Ian's
Braver than you' I heard my Auntie say. So why was I crying?

4. *Walking Along*

This walking. Funny business. One foot in front of the other, a
slow and shifting dance that never changes. Once saw a vicar fall
flat on his back in the ice. Once saw an old bloke fallen down in
the road, waving his stick and shouting HEYOP. Once saw a milk
float turn a corner a bit sharply and all the milk crates fell off very
slowly making a crashing sound that went on and on and then
the milkman got out of the float and said DOES THA WANT
SOME MILK? Once found a ten bob note on the floor and stuck
it in my pocket and bloke came past and he looked sad so I said
HAVE YOU LOST A TEN BOB NOTE? And he said THAT I
HAVE YOUNG UN and I gave it to him and only years later,
years later, did I realise he was lying. One foot in front of the other.

5. *Snow Hill/Snape Hill/Those White Christmas Card Envelopes*

In the snow, this could be anywhere but it is here, a place
Defined by footprints, by the snow in the face, by the white
Of the Christmas card envelopes I'm clutching. My hat is black

In the white space I'm floating through. My glasses are made
Of snow and they magnify the flakes; my ears are full of snow
And they magnify the sound of the snow falling until it sounds

Like the playing of a vast melting instrument made of snow.
My card envelopes are white flags and I'm slipping, falling
Over in slow motion, Kong off the snowy Empire State Building,

A scarecrow collapsing, a tree falling in a wood and nobody
Can hear. I fall down in the snow and a tear of blood
Spots the white…

6. *Cold Walk: Snape Hill December*

Breath hangs like history; shoes slip on the ice
That grew overnight like a plant, a plant called ice
Or a moss that you might have called ice

That took you back to childhood, the sound
You made when you slipped on it, a sound
Like the word. Ice! You said, making a sound

That carried all the way down Snape Hill
And bounced off the walls on the hill
And echoed and came back up hill

Back up through history where the breath hangs;
Short trousers, school jumper, hair hangs
Loose from the face, sky where a moon hangs
So close you could walk to it through the ice.

7. *As an Old Man Ian Remembers His Walks*

I remember remembering, and the remembering, remember,
was what got me thinking about the walks. The dog. Blackpool Tower.
The bloke shouting Help. The Moon, and then I remembered

things that never happened on the walk: the laughing clown,
the bloke that stopped me and said 'Is this the road to Birkenhead?'
and all his mates in the car laughed. Now I sit

in a chair all day and I think about that walk and I wish that I was
on it,
I wish that I was on it now but they're just bringing me some tea
some nice tea. Some nice tea that I could take on the walk.

The Evening of the Day Pavarotti Died

I poured some Carnation Milk into a cup of coffee
And sat outside to watch the light fading
On the tree in the cemetery at the back of our garden.

My wife couldn't get over it. 'You never have milk
In coffee, do you?' she said. She often
Ends her sentences with the rising hint of a question.

We both listened and from Mr Lowe's house next door
And from Steve's house up the street we heard
The last note of Nessun Dorma rising and hanging

There like light on a tree. If you want perfection, come here:
The tree, the note, and yes, even the Carnation Milk
In the coffee in the bright blue cup. Then the squirrel

On the shed was too much, like an orchestra taking
One too many bows when you've already stood up to go.

Drift

1. *All The Coal Ever Dug from Flack's Mine*

Solid black cloud hanging in the sky.
Island in a sea of ten fields.
Wagon after wagon after wagon after wagon until this paper ends.
Heat of a small black star.
Infinite shovels full.
A hill, burning.
It waits in the air all across England.
One big lump or seventeen billion smaller lumps: you decide.

2. *Pit Ghosts*

Ghosts of all the men who ever worked here,
However briefly. Ten years, one day. No matter;
They are still here, still in the pit
Like those shadow puppets your children make.

Ghosts of all the human sounds ever made here.
Shout. Laugh. Cough. Joke. Argument. Song. Warning.
Fart. List. Yell. Grunt. Sneeze. Hey. Here. What? What?
What? Watch! Whoa! Where? Eee. Ow! Shit! Mm. M. m.

Ghost of all the coal dug from here by hands and shovels;
It's in the air, somewhere. It has been formed. It has been dug.
It has been burned. It waits, in the air.

Ghost faces in the pit light. Ghost mouths in the pit light.

3. *Pitman Speyks*

Nowt else suits. Desk job, security man
In a daft hat. No chance. Mucky and filthy
And some bastard nicked the showers but still

Nowt else suits. Diggin and back brokken
Every neet. Fingers hurtin. Neck hurtin.
Head hurtin. But what else could I do, eh?

Shelf stackin? Driving a wagon, delivering stuff?
Serving tea? Taxi driving: where duz tha want ter gu
Madam? No chance. Nowt else suits.

4. The Back, Bent

In the half-dark
In the half-bent
Light, the back
Bends, half-aware
Of the dull pain
Of repetition, history.

In the half-light
The back, bending
In the half-awake
Light, the back
Bending, half-awash
With the harsh pain
Of history, memory.

In the half-gleam
The back, bent.
The back glistens
With half-sweat,
Half-dirt; bends,
Listens for half-shifts
In the earth above;
Ear bent, rock-sweat.

5. The Mine Sings

(Note: if you go to the mine late at night with recording
equipment, you will hear singing. This is the old and very rare
phenomenon of PitVoice, heard occasionally through the ages
from bellpits in Scotland to Silver Mines in Cornwall. The words
can be indistinct, but I've transcribed them as well as I can. Sadly
my pen (a free one that I nicked from a room in a posh hotel)
wouldn't work so I had to get the words as best I could by writing
with coal on the lap of my white shirt.)

Open mouth, take in air
Sound of shovel (.............) coal shifting
Black night of the underground

Boots, lights on hard, hard hats
And the voices, the (.............) voices
Melting into pick on stone

Pull fire from face, fire from face
(.............) in the eyes
Eyes of the mine. Singing.

Did You Ask for a Decaff off that Other Lady?

(0600 Newcastle to King's Cross)
The woman opposite me is tearing CVs into half, into quarters,
                    into eighths, into confetti, into dust that

Catches the light
A staple gleams
A staple! Gleams
A! Staple gleams
A staple gleams!
'My experience includes:

Inventing new names for tree-trunks & eating wheelbarrows.'
Oops! There I go!
Quartered/confetti'd/dusted!
'My education is
Mainly in the School of Mud and the
Academy of Chips and Red Sauce.'
Okay, I'll tear myself. (CVs scatter table like salt.)
Would
You
Like
My
Gleaming
Staple?
Have you noticed how flat the Fens are and how my chins
Wobwobble.
Sorry? You aren't (list)ening.
'I have travelled widely beyond Worksop'
'My hobbies include foot- table- crick- ches- domin-'
Sound of a zipped bag.

Yorkshire Pudding Rules

The tin must not gleam. Must never be new.
If there is dried sweat somewhere in its metal
It must be your mother's. The flour must be strong
And white as the face of Uncle Jack
When he came back from the desert. The eggs
Must come from an allotment. The allotment
Must belong to your father-in-law.
The eggs have to be broken
With one swift movement over the bowl.
If there is dried sweat somewhere in its Pyrex
It must be your mother's. The milk
Must have been delivered by Colin Leech
At 0430. The fork has to be an old one. The wrist

Must, simply must, ache after the mixing.
The flour must introduce itself to the yolk of the egg.
The egg has to be allowed to talk to the flour.
The milk must dance with them both: foxtrot, then quickstep.
The pepper must be scattered, black on off-white.
The oven must be hotter than ever.
The lard has to come in a tight white pack.
The lard must almost catch fire in the oven.
The oven door must open and you must shout
JESUS CHRIST as the heat smacks you in the chops.

Follow these rules
And the puddings will rise to heaven
And far beyond.

A Series of Novels

1. My dad on a farm in Lanarkshire in 1929. He sails across a
pond in a boat he's made himself and decides he wants to go to
sea.
2. My dad walks home the four miles from school with a prize he's
won for an essay he wrote on the League of Nations.
3. My dad in the navy in 1937. He sees shoals of flying fish from
the back of the boat.
4. My dad in his cabin in a storm. The boat is lurching and he has
to be very careful as he sticks his stamps in his album.
5. My dad carrying a drunk sailor out of a brothel in Shanghai in
1940.
6. My dad, home from sea for the last time in 1958, carries me
into the garden. I say gogn gogn gogn.
7. My dad in the conservatory tying fishing flies in 1977. He says
the names out loud. Bloody butcher, baby doll.
8. My dad sits on the bedroom floor, his face twisted to one side.
No problem, he says. No problem.

Black Cloud Over My House Sometime in the 1960s

Look, that cloud
Black as Emma Peel's leather trousers
On our black and white television
In that front room with a canary in the corner. Emma,

Maybe trousers isn't the right word. Pants. Skin.
That cloud seems tight, full, tight. My voice
Is cracking at the edges

And there's a single hair on my chest
like a wire or a spider's thigh. I
showed it to our John and he laughed.

Saturday night. Me and Emma, in the front room.
And our John. And my Dad. And my Mam.
And the canary, singing. And my single hair. And her trousers.

My dad joins me in the garden.
There'll be a cloudburst soon he says, his voice lilting.

The Inevitability of Snow

The inevitability of snow
The predictability of the way
That frost forms

The changeability of clouds
The shifting quality of your breath
In the air

One flake in the air
As the year turns
stars reflected

In a midnight lake
The stability of the moon
Except when it waxes

The stability of the moon
Except when it wanes
The mobility of the moon

Except when it never moves
Or never seems to move.
The unpredictability of the moon.

Chorus:
The inevitability of snow
The predictability of the way

That frost forms
The visible signs of your breath;
The scarf of air that hangs.

The human steam of talking
In the evening.
The way that winter hangs on

The pockets of filthy snow.
The snowman reduced to a scarf.
The ice on the garden, waiting.

Chorus:
The inevitability of snow
The predictability of the way
That frost forms

The inevitability of snow
The temporary nature of footprints
The blizzard that blocked off your glasses.
The blackbird in the naked tree.
The light of a gritter from far away, turning and turning.
The last bus going up the hill at walking pace.

The man at the bus stop texting somebody.
The girl at the bus stop texting somebody.
The inevitability of snow.
The inevitability of snow.

The Idea of Loneliness in the Little Chef, Uttoxeter

Morning is an egg. Morning is a slice of toast.
Morning is a spoon that he looks into,
Seeing his face upside down.

His suit, his tie. The screensaver children
On the laptop. The egg. The toast.
He purses his lips and

He is about to whistle
Or he is about to kiss the air.
The screensaver children

The bright morning sun.
He is pursing his lips
His lips his lips his lips.

Platform 2

We are both waiting and he comes over to me,
His cap is dark. *I found my dad*

He says, as though he knows me. *Good* I say,
That's good. His cap, his cap is dark.

At stair bottom Ian. He'd hung hissen.
His cap, his cap, his cap is dark.

*He must have been low, Ian, to do that
Does tha think?* His cap, his cap, his cap, his

Cap is dark. *I allus get a return ticket,
Just in case.* His cap, his cap, his cap, his cap

You know the rest

Aubade/Nocturne

You decide. It's your choice.
I was just putting some *ideas*
Into a bag to take to the Charity Shop,
Tha noz. Just a few *concepts*
and an argument or two.

Day or night? Who can tell?
Light comes through the
Curtains they're that thin.
Light allus comes through.
I suppose it's a lifestyle choice

Ont' part of t' curtains. Trouble
Is, then, a few weeks later,
Because they have to wash 'em,
And bag 'em and that, I see
Folks walking down Wombwell

Wearing my *ideas*, my *concepts*.
That old *argument* of mine doesn't
Fit that bloke in the baseball cap
But he's still wearing it. Too tight pal.
Tha wants to chuck the chips. Yes,

But not all over me. Funny. Is it day
Or night then, eh? Got yer! Here,
Try this *idea* on for size. It's coming
Back into fashion, kid. Day or night?
You tell me. Just tell me. Tell me.

The Poet Speaks

I'M TAKING FRENCH WITH MATH!
I FIGURE THAT MAY HELP ME TO STOP SHOUTING!
THE FRENCH POETRY IS REALLY DEEP!
THE MATH IS COMPLEX BUT, HEY, REWARDING!
I LIKE JACCOTTET BEST!
HIS POETRY IS BASED ON NATURE AND HE'S SWISS,
                                    NOT FRENCH!
SWISS PLUS FRENCH EQUALS POETRY!
IT ALL ADDS UP!

Unrealismus/Realismus

You-choose-it!
It's the classic lineup:
Ian McMillan, piano
Ian McMillan, bass
Ian McMillan, drums

1. The Short-Lived South Lanarkshire Silent Film Industry

The year is 1926 and my dad is walking to school down a lane; a
man in a beret leaps out from behind a tree and shouts to my dad
down a megaphone. My dad is frightened but the man seeks to
reassure him. 'Just need ya for the action scene, kiddo. Just need
ya t'walk across the frame' 'How can you walk across a frame?' my
dad asks, but the man in the beret is shouting at a group of people
who are dressed as clowns. One is smoking and the man with
the beret rips the cigarette from his mouth and flings it in the air
where it turns and turns and turns.

2. Visiting the Cemetery Last Saturday[1]

You carry the flowers, two bunches
£2.00 each from Morrisons

I carry the scissors, and the cloth
And we turn onto the path

And walk down past the chapel of rest
And the air feels much fresher than yesterday.

My mam and dad are buried next door but one
To your dad, separated by one stone,

Mr. Bielby. I pass you the scissors and
You snip, snip, snip the ends

---

1 depending when you read this, of course

Of the flowers. You snip, you arrange
And a blackbird makes a sudden lunge

To the ground near that accident victim.
I bag the scissors, the cloth. We go home.

Ah've Soiled Ma Breeks!

(2012)

Come and Sit Over Here with Those Ideas of Yours

To be honest, the surprise of a poem coming
Is like when you go to see a documentary
Followed by a talk from the director
And it turns out to be a musical.

Or when you go *Hey! Somebody's*
Put flamin' sugar in me tea!

Or when you go *Why didn't you tell mi*
Yer could see mi vest through mi shirt?

Each morning on my walk I pass a man in a cap;
We nod and he raises his cap. We pass each other,
Our nods hang in the air like two feathers. The poem,
The moment of the poem, has passed by. Feathers,
Hanging, falling, floating. But not flying. Not flying.

Ah've Soiled Ma Breeks!

Start wi' this: kitchen light, slatted through blinds
On a Friday morning's opening statement of intent.
Soundtrack is avant-garde jazz squealing and groaning
From an iPad's mouth: a man in armour is falling downstairs,
It seems, and it's making him whistle and punch a 'cello.

Ian's plunging the plunger on a pot of black coffee.
The best bit of drinking it is plunging the plunger. Plunge,
Ian. Wait now. Let it stand. Try not to think of the apples.
The slatted light alters slightly: it's the postlady with a parcel
To sign for. 'What's that row?' she says, nodding at the noise.

Ian signs. He's thinking of a reply but she's gone. Pour. Slurp.
Now he can think of the apples. Feral apples, he calls them,
The ones you see hanging on trees by the side of the road,
By the railway line as the train slows down. Red and green stop
And go signs you can make pies with. And today Ian is going,

With a carrier bag from ALDI, to pick some. Pour, slurp. The
Jazz increases in volume and intensity: now two alligators
Are fighting over the ownership of a gate that needs oiling
And that music forms a bumpy bridge to the next section
Of this poem, where Ian is scrambling down to a hedge

By the A635 between Darfield and Ardsley with his carrier
Bag. A passing artisan in a car shouts through an open window
'Your poems are shite!' to the scrambling bard and a crow caws.
Ian bends and picks red ferals from the floor, picks red ferals
From a branch, ignores the feeling of tightness in a place

That he'd rather not think about. Ah, the joy of the feral apple-
Collector and the avant-garde music fan, carrier-bagging
The beauties as tractors fields away and that crow and apple-
Landing-in-bag sounds combine to make a music that should,
Really should, win awards. Too much coffee. He needs a wee,

So let's let the avant-garde music swell again to take us
To the next location for this poem. Actually, it's a double
Scene, so the music will resemble the mixing of Yorkshire
Puddings with the shattering of a stained-glass window
By a robot seagull. Scene: a village in the Scottish Borders,

My dad emerging with a smile and an upthumb from a toilet
At the back of a garage. It's the mid 1970s, so the attendants
Still served you and one of them's smiling. Dad's zip is still open.
Scene: a hospital room. My dad is slumped. His stroke has stroked
Him. But not like a lover. He looks past me and says, in a voice

Far away in the distance: 'Ah've soiled ma breeks!' Music is
Rising and now it's a storm at sea as described by a Martian
And it takes us to the next part of the poem where Ian's walking
As fast as he can down the A635. A jogger passes and shouts
'Soon be time for a cuppa!' The music stays under

This next bit as Ian walks faster, thinking of deserts and
Sand dunes and a box of dry lentils. The postlady waves
from her passing van. Don't wave, you bugger! Give
Me a lift! Time is measured in water, I suppose. You start
As a trickle of a stream in the high hills and you grow and

Mature into a wide river and people use you for pleasure
And work and they splash around in you or they gaze
Into you looking for reflections of themselves. And eventually
You overflow your banks. You overflow your banks. You
Almost make it. You get to the door. It's locked. You

Stagger round the back, into the garden. You almost make it.
You are carrying red feral apples in an ALDI bag and you almost
Make it. How much of an inland patio sea can a few cups
Of coffee make? More than you think. Ah've soiled ma breeks.
Let the music enter a thoughtful phase: let it sound like fruit.

Anchored

My dad is sitting in his chair, and he's at sea. His eyes are casting out over some vast horizon. Jackie waves from next door; she's hanging out the washing, but my dad is sitting in his chair, and he's at sea. He won't be moving from the chair till the carer comes and then the movements will be painful and there may be water in the chair, and under it. I tell myself it's seawater. I tell him it's seawater. Jackie's sheets flap like sails. She waves cheerfully to him but he only sees the flapping of a great gull's wings. When the carer's been I'll ask my dad to tell me about the sinking of the Bismarck again. His eyes will brim with seawater. There'll be fish under his chair. Jackie will sit in her garden and she'll feel her lawn rippling. The sea swells with my dad's voice. Jackie's lawn rises and falls. There are guns in the distance, flashes of guns.

A Scientific Explanation of the Mystery of the Passing of Time

There was no lipstick on the mug
She had her cup-a-soup in. A
Sudden motorbike on the top road
Broke the silence. *Last night I heard an
Owl* he says. *An owl. An owl.*

The choral music on the radio
Is so soft I can hardly hear it.
The mug is resting on a mat
From Argentina: *Tango is*

A three-minute short story
That man said to me that time
In Buenos Aires. Yes, pal.
I b'leeve ee. I b'leeeve ee.

Tony Bought a Guitar and Got a Parking Fine

This happened in Retford. Trains pass
Through Retford at speed but Tony and I
Had time to kill. Charity shops. A café
Where the silvery teapot reflected my face.

Another charity shop. I flicked through
Paperbacks: Gervase Phinn, Captain Corelli.
But Tony saw the guitar. Oh, Tony, surely
Not? But he did. And by now it was ten past two.

We rushed. His guitar twanged in the air.
We got back to the car just too late, too late.
Tony shouted. There was unseasonal heat
For October. He flung the ticket to the Retford floor

And I opened my mouth and said a daft thing
And my face turned red in the afternoon sun.
First silvery. Now red. Trains pass through. They're gone.
Tony flailed at the strings in a heartbroken song.

Tony kippered the strings in a heartbroken song.
Tony rinsed out the strings in heartbroken song.
Tony light-greened the strings in a heartbroken song.
Tony teatowelled the strings in a heartbroken song.

The Language of Philosophical Enquiry

To be fair you know it's like that old sort of saying
'If an electric toothbrush falls over in an empty bathroom
Is there a sound?' Sort of the idea of the toothbrush
You know clipping the sink before it hits the floor
But if you're not there if you're I don't know up
In the loft or something daft like that sorting out

Your old Green Lantern comics, cataloguing them
In a manner of speaking, is there a you know noise?
Any happening, any happening then: tap on, lav flush,
Light string click, bee banging into the sort of window,
Cistern filling, pipes you know kind of kind of bumping
And nobody's like there is there a noise sort of thing?

Trumping doesn't count. Don't be stupid. Somebody's
Got to be there for a sort of trumping noise. But to be fair
If the bathroom's empty and the sort of noise kind of happens
Is there a noise? Have you got an inhaler I could borrow?
A blue one. Or yes a brown one would be fine. Absolutely.

Early Morning Stroll. Deep Woods. Just Seen My Mate
Who Spent His Early Years in a Children's Home.

Grass and bracken grabbing my trouser leg,
Slip-slipping up this 'hill' that used to be the stack
Of Mitchell's Main. Trees have names, birds (like
That little shep/spuggy/flap-bastard there)
Have names, clouds have, well, cloud-names

So my gasps for air should have names. That
Throat-clearer, ur-language, grunty-grimace.
That inhaler-sound, deflatin' balloon. That
Half-HEYOP, half exasper-bubble. That sigh-that-

Could-be-the-uncle-of-a-crisp-packet-scrunch.
That whisper sonata. That last word in a lost
And forgotten language that only lasted for
An hour, anyway. I should name them all.
Then I should write them down. Then I should

Set them to music.

Face of Our Lord Jesus Christ
Seen in Yorkshire Pudding

Some called it a miracle, and I could appreciate
The infinite pity in the eyes, but I preferred
To think of that face of that woman I saw that time,

Pressed against that window of that small house
In that Northern town as my train slowed
At the bottom of her long back garden. Her lawn

Was ragged and tired, and the trampoline looked
Recently jumped on. Planning permission's
Been applied for: shops and a sixty-bedroom hotel

And a visitor centre lit from above so the pudding
Can be as visible as possible. When I looked at it
I thought it seemed as though Our Lord was wearing a tie.

They're advertising for a Poet In Residence. Even
From a distance I could tell she'd been crying. A tricycle,
A doll's leg, a garden chair with a kettle on it, a

Right mess that garden was and no mistake, no mistake.
I might apply. I've written about Yorkshire Puddings before.
The train waited for a while and then moved slowly. She waved.

A man said he thought he saw the face of Our Lord in the Pudding
Wink. Now that would be a miracle. A miracle of irony and
Self-knowledge. I'll write some pudding haiku and pin 'em

To my CV, send 'em off. Can't hurt. Can't do any harm.

Ian McMillan's Unfishnished Poem

They found it in his shoe, after his sudden collapse
Just outside the Tesco Extra in Wombwell. 'Loosen
His shoes!' shouted a stallholder in the open market

And a passer-by loosened Ian's left shoe, hoping against
Hope against hope it would help him to breathe.
The unfishnished poem was scrunched up in the shoe,

And that bloke who used to be the security man
At the tennis-ball factory held it up and read it, aloud,
To the small gathering. It was a bit like a poetry reading.

A glass container
Shining in the light
Of a half-bar electric fire

The crowd murmured. 'If you're going to leave an
Unfishnished poem, make it a good 'un!' said that woman
Who was related to that woman who lived in Jump.

T'invisible Man O' Methley

From Yorksheer Legends, *Methley Monthly Publications, 1912*

They seek him here, they seek him theer, they seek him every
Methley-wheer, that Jack O't'Hedge, that Will o't' wisp, that
no-bloke, that cap-hung-on-nowt, that see-through chap, that
empty glass, that breeze ruffling yer muffler, that hole in t'street.

They seek him here, they seek him theer, they seek him every
Methley-wheer, that absent kid in t'schoolroom, that free seat
at t'evening scran, that shadder by't' winder that's not a shadder
o'nothin' at all.

They seek him here, they seek him theer, they seek him every
Methley-wheer, that rustlin' o't' curtains in a freezin' parlour, that
throyt cleared in an attic where nobody's ivver bin, that sprite, that
elf, that boggart, that what-the-ummer.

They should hev looked i'mi shed. Ah've gorrim. Ah feed 'im bacon.

Torch Passes By

Torch passes by old men, slow on street corners.
Torch passes by them. They say nothing. They nod.
Torch passes by. Dickie Bird's statue gleams in the sun.
Torch passes by children who pause in their laughter.
Torch passes by them. They wave slightly. They gaze.
Torch passes by. Oakwell's floodlights flare briefly. A test.
Torch passes by women who wait for the next bus.
Torch passes by them. They photo. They txt.
Torch passes by. At Old Moor a rare bird pauses, sings.
Torch passes by lads who are comparing biceps.
Torch passes by them. Their CVs glow brighter.
Torch passes by. Barnsley Main's headgear is history-rusted.
Torch passes by crowds who are cheering and shouting.
Torch passes by them. The cheering grows fainter.
Torch passes by. Torch passes by. Torch passes by.

A Black Dog in Four Legs

1. *First leg, this is the first leg*

Low mist, a low mist kissing the fields
Dawn is making its mind up
Whether to break or not
Break or not

Prints
In the
Snow

This is the time between
Waking and sleeping
Living and dying
Yesterday and tomorrow

Prints
In the
Snow

High moon, High moon shines in the sky
Night simply just can't decide
Whether to stay or go
Stay or go

And the black dog is pressing
prints
In the snow

2. *Second leg, this is the second leg*

Mam, I saw it. I saw it!

I saw The Black Dog
Through the late-night chip shop window
Someone had drawn a face in the steam
And the black dog pressed his nose close

Mam, I saw it. I saw it!

I saw The Black Dog
The other morning in the back yard
Someone had hung my vest on the line
And the black dog ran behind it

Mam, I saw it. I saw it!

I saw The Black Dog
Turning midnight by the gravestones
Someone had been buried yesterday
And the black dog's eyes were gleaming

3. *Third leg, this is the third leg*

What time is it, Mr. Dog?
What time?

Jaws stick
Together

Paws click
On the road
Icy weather

What time is it, Mr. Dog?
What time?

Clock ticks
Through the night
And a single feather
Floats…
What time is it, Mr Dog?

It's Black Dog O'Clock…

4. *Fourth leg, this is the fourth leg*

Mam I saw it in the dark
Eyes like torches, teeth like stars
At the far side of the park
Where the bad lads wreck the cars
They stole…

It's nearly Black Dog O'Clock!

Mam I heard its freezing cry
Hanging scary in the air
It can run or it can fly
It can find you anywhere
At all.

It's nearly Black Dog O'Clock!

The Black Dog: I believe in it,
Even when the room is light and the telly's on
The Black Dog: I believe in it,
Even when my granddad laughs and says the dog's gone…

Mam I heard its time tick tock
Moving from the day to night
This hour is now Black Dog O'Clock
Darkness soaking into light…

It's nearly Black Dog O' Clock!
It's nearly Black Dog O' Clock!

Dream of a Tree in a Spanish Graveyard from a Small House in The South Yorkshire Coalfield

Hold this piece of wood to your ear and listen: gunfire.
Hold this piece of wood to your ear and listen: that music.

The actors paused briefly and glanced at the director,
Hoping for the word. Up above the sun burned like a reminder
That their life was passing. The director barked 'Cut!'

Hold this piece of wood to your ear and listen: silence follows.
Hold this piece of wood to your ear and listen: time slips sideways.

You and your brother and your mother and your father
Watching the telly, breath held. Up above the light flickered,
A reminder of the men working below. Your dad said 'Well...'

Hold this piece of wood to your ear and listen: cage slowing
Hold this piece of wood to your ear and listen: pits closing.

At the end of the film your brother fires an imaginary gun
At the lightshade. Outside the pit bus rumbles to North Street
With the good and the bad and the ugly on board.

Hold this piece of wood to your ear and listen:
Hold this piece of wood to your ear and listen:
Hold this piece of wood to your ear and listen:
It's just a dream of a tree in a Spanish graveyard...

M' Writing Table

I reach behind the curtain for it every morning. I know, I
know, that old reaching-behind-the-curtain thing, so loaded
with the kind of resonance you can just about taste: hotel
rooms to see where the ummer you are today,

lusty non-gent grabbing into the shower, boiled-ham actor
peeping to see what the audience look like tonight and they
always look like bashed neeps,

but grab it anyway, from behind the curtain, put it up,
clicking the legs into upright, the legs that your wife says
won't last much longer well just let them last long enough to
finish this, maybe just last long enough

to start the next one. Come on, table, come on. Hold up.
Hold up. And what the hecky are you staring at? Move
along, please, nothing to see here. Nothing to see.

Medium pulling summat from behind the veil,

Playing Chess with Uncle Charlie

Well, for a start he called it *chest*
And he said that any piece
Could move in any direction and take
Any other piece in any way it wanted to

Including flicking them off the board
Or wrapping them in a rubber band.

He'd change from black to white
On a whim, and once he made a hill of sugar
On the corner square *for that castle thing*
To hide behind he said, his eyes big

Behind those glasses that magnified
So much for so long with such love.

Once we were playing in the back room;
He'd just substituted a Park Drive for a pawn
And he was singing along to *Sing Something Simple*
So it must have been Sunday, and in the kitchen

Unknown to us, my Auntie had just glugged
From a bleach bottle, thinking it was lemonade.

He was holding forth, continuing my political education:
Bevan got it right, Ian: lower than vermin.
That's what they are, Tories, lower than vermin.
And he put my king in his waistcoat pocket

And said *Checkity mate, Ian. Checkity mate.*
In the kitchen my Auntie was gasping for breath.

Uncle Charlie couldn't read or write,
Left school too soon, straight down the pit.
I once tried to teach him, but my Janet and John
Embarrassed us both so we got the chessboard

Out and never mentioned it again. He
Put a hat on the bishop, made from an eggshell.

Plain, Cheese & Onion, Salt & Vinegar

Nobody knew what the terrible smell was
Until Geoff pointed out it was Uncle Charlie
letting whang.

He was just a presence then, Charlie
A shape on the downstairs bed
Waft that Mirror, will yer?

Reduced to a pair of
Glasses and a pair of braces
Who's boffed? Charlie.

Spitting bright green phlegm
Onto the banked fire
Like a hoss!

Or into a selection
Of empty crisp bags.

Fantasia on a Theme of Uncle Charlie

'I'll tell you this, Ian lad, Nye Bevan…'
And the shattered lungs would draw in air, English air,
In that back room in North Street,
'I'll tell you this, Ian lad…' Breath wheezing

Like somebody scraping pit boots on the path,
And the coughing would start, and his old themes
Would fight their way through the dust
'I'll tell you this, Ian lad, Nye Bevan…'

Voice trying to lift like English strings lifting
In a concert hall, voice breaking your heart
Like those strings break my heart every time,
'I'll tell you this, Ian. Nye Bevan got it right…'

Uncle Charlie. Your theme. Your fantasies
On your own theme. Heard you telling your mates
When you walked home from the pit.
When you could still walk. 'I'll tell you this, Ian lad…'

Uncle Jack's Rubber Tarts, Boxing Day 1964

Better get the poem written quickly,
Before the rubber tarts come out.

We've had tea. We're just having a bun
Or a tart before we go home from Marlcliffe Road.

Uncle Jack is talking about when he saw
The American General Mark Clark

Driving the wrong way, away from the fighting,
Back in '42 or '43. He can't remember or won't

Which year. *Ah sez to him, nar den, General
Mark Clark, feytin's dat way da noz. Da guin*

Wrong way fo't feytin. The Sheffield 'A's
Make the name Mark Clarke ring like a bell.

Hurry up. Tarts will be out soon. *Ar. A flirted wi't
Communist party. We all did. Nar den: would yer*

Like a tart befoor yer gu? Too late. Rubber tarts
Are out. Bite them. Bite them. Outside, snow falls

Like a reminder that language is always going to be
The battleground. The fighting is that way, you know.

The Sun Comes Up

The sun comes up like a sidekick in a gangster film
Across the glacier's teatowel folds. I thought this island
Was uninhabited, and then I saw the mirror.

The mirror with me in it. Listen: country music,
Pure as sellotape, rhythmic as Wednesday, that Wednesday
You told me I was as easy to read as a comic.

I had a reader's letter in The Dandy. I had a reader's
Letter in the Beano. Did you have a reader's letter
In the Beezer? Now you're being naive.

A Mo-ment

Strictly not a mo-ment, but a mo-mentette
Or a shard-of-a-sec, a time-bit. Found a black
Hair amongst the grey, a pencil-line in the silver

In a split of Time, a second cracked like a pavement
And I thought 'I'm getting younger. I'm
A time-machine. Goodbye, middle-age, hello

Youth!' Strictly not a mo-ment, but a CRUSHED SEC,
A grain o' sand in an egg-timer. No matter: one black
Hair on my grey head. Time reversing like a drunk

In a stolen JCB. Get the junior school cap
from the drawer,
Mr. Mc!

My Achilles, He'll

Moment between sleep-village and awake-village
Is when language puts on a hatt tthatt doesn't fit.

And at that mo you look into YE abyss of what it'll
Be like later, in your 80s/90s. Word-marmalade

That you can't spread on the gob's toast, no matter
How hard you try. Thinky-foot won't go into action-slipper

And who is that speaking? And what are they saying?
And will those biscuits that the wise call Poetry

Help you now? Bit of a lighthouse in YE darkness,
Bit of a map in YE maples lanes an roads? Hope so,

Really hope so, but you can't tell. You only need an
Umbrella when it's raining. Get me? My drift?

Keith's Mankini: A Three-Line Work in Progress

Draft 7
Eating fried eggs in it is 'interesting', especially
When it comes to the dipping of the bread
And the looking at the clock *at the same time*

Draft 11
Fried egg chewing comes easy, not so
The crumb-shower. Eggy bread, eggy mankini,
Eggy   *time*

Draft 36
The egg somehow became the mankini,
So much was spilled, so much time was lost
So much 'time' was 'lost'

Draft 78
The mankini was called Keith and the man
Who wore the mankini was called Keith
And the house he lived in was called Keith

Draft 134
Egg Keith. EggKini. *Egg Time.*
Dipped bread as signifier.
Tight mankini as remote control FOR YOUR LIFE, KEITH!

Jazz Peas

(2014)

Me and Dave and Thelonious Monk
Waiting for the 14 Bus

Another Friday evening in Dave Sunderland's front room.
Another new LP bought in the jazz section of Casa Disco.
Another night when Dave's mam was out at the Chapel.

Turn it up, Dave, turn it
Right up. Turn the lights out, Dave
And let's wait.

Another track on the Underground album: Ugly Beauty.
Another rearrangement of time and space and coincidence.
Another listen, Dave. Put it on again, mate. Soon be time.

In the front room dark
We try to snap our fingers
And it sounds like rain on a soft roof.

Another few moments to wait, if the 14 bus is on time.
Another double-decker light/modern jazz moment.
Another adolescent evening spent wishing we could leave here.

Round the corner by The Station Inn,
The 14 bus; Monk's music redefines
So much, so much. The 14's lights light
Up the room, sweep over it, away.

Another hour to wait before the next 14 bus, Dave.
Another biscuit from the tin. Let's pretend it's a whisky biscuit.
Another magical moment, Dave: Thelonious, the 14, the light.

Play it again, until your mam
Comes in. She said she was bringing chips
And mushy peas. We'll pretend they're
Jazz peas, Dave; jazz peas.

An Archaeologist Finds an Umbrella

Not a particularly old one,
At the dig's edge.

Left from a night out,
Blown outside in

And chucked on the floor
Like a flower clipped

From a bunch. The archaeologist
Made a thing of opening it,

Stood there, half a brolly
Above her head like a fossil.

And it wasn't even raining.
Now try and guess

What this says about the past.

Annual Report

Poem are not big employers, poems are
SMEs. We gather by the watercooler
and we discuss, lyrically, how many
watercooler moments make a watercooler

hour. Poems import and export at the same time
and every day's an AGM or an EGM
or a Genda. Any other business ? No,
no other business but this one. Making do

with the old machinery alongside the new
and the machinery that you make yourself,
that you discard after one pressing, one smelting,

Approaching those 'Ruddy' Belisha Beacons Near the Post Office Again

You can see them from a long way off,
From when you pass the half-visible ponies
In the field where the school was

By the bus shelter with the bloke in it,
The bloke whose face is lit by his iPhone
Like a tallow-maker's face is lit in an old master.

One Belisha Beacon off. One Belisha Beacon on.
Small parcels of light sent first class to each other;
Moons chucking glowing balls across the road's net.

A car slows by the Post Office and a woman jumps out
And gives me a letter. 'Can tha stick this int' box for mi?'
She asks. I will, in a minute. Jogger walks by, gasping-gasp.

First I'll hold the envelope up to the Belisha Beacon.
Not to read the letter inside, you understand,
Just to gaze at light on paper, light on writing.

As Thoughs

As though morning has ting-tinged its glass with a fork to get us
to listen.

As though a turtle suddenly began to sprint urgently across the
beach and thousands of other turtles followed, some playing
instruments.

As though somebody, a lighthouse keeper say, woke up and began
speaking in a dead language.

As though a misplaced apostrophe really is the sentence's sequin,
there to be admired an'd loved.

As though the zebra is not an animal but a memory.

As though trembling is the new black.

As though TV remotes and egg-cups were all that remained of
civilisation.

As though austerity was an anagram not a solution.

As though a tree's rings were thought to be a travel journal until
Steven told us the truth that Thursday.

As though The Queen did robot dancing in private.

As though all memories triggered by the raising of umbrellas had
to be discounted by law.

As though the CEO would gladly pay for the dustman's child to
go to university.

As though search engines only found strawberries.

As though a mirror was a map that took you nowhere every day of
your life.

As though Sunday wasn't a day but a pebble in your sock.

As though hoot and hoot and hoot and hoot sound very different
to owls.

As though austerity was a fence not a caged bird's song.

As though the Moon is a piece of hotel soap.

As though King Lear is a fly-on-the-wall documentary.

As though thanking bus drivers is a new inert gas.

As though the fascinator is a symphonic poem.

As though the 27th and 28th letters of the alphabet could only be
represented by rubber bands or worms.

As though a gravestone could ever be subtle/improvised/smoked.

As though after fingernails your death keeps growing.
As though a fat-cat can be used as a flotation device.
As though thread and needle are the only things you'll ever need to
climb a mountain.
As though a hat is adequate.
As though the doorbell in your heart rings and rings.
As though your visit to the First World War Battlefields was
arranged during the First World War by mistake.
As though punctuation was edible in Tudor times.
As though when a balloon bursts a tiny button of time begins to
rust.
As though all the nails in the world disappeared and reappeared on
the Isle of Man.
As though enjoyment has its own contours and descants and
ladder-rungs.
As though the King Of Sardinia lived in my pocket.
As though a tattoo could think, dream and knit.
As though a steep hill always stumbles and falls as the sun sets.
As though her fingernail knew something it wasn't letting on.
As though a circus tent can always be relied on for fog and the
runic alphabet.
As though austerity is a colour chart.
As though, in certain religions, the soul is represented in frescoes
as a monocle.
As though soup can dream.
As though there is always a navy behind every settee.
As though the phrase 'bench of grapes' could ever, ever, be wrong.
As though a small plane hits turbulence like Tuesday hits
Wednesday.
As though Time is shaped like a tench.
As though Dracula spoke in one of the available
Northamptonshire accents.
As though there is a constellation called Austerity that has no stars,
just buckets.
As though 'My elevator has broken' is the 346th most common
phrase in the language.
As though translation will always be perfectt.
As though matching luggage is what led to the correct analysis of
Stonehenge's shadow.

As though tartan is The Devil's Blush.
As though, at The Last Supper, there was no pepper.
As though He Who Has a Zip in His Back has The Secret.
As though lizards communicate through flamenco-like stamping.
As though truth is warm.
As though The Great American Songbook is a bungalow.
As though, in the end, nothing depended on the red wheelbarrow.
As though the tide really just goes out and out.
As though the bell that signals the start of a new round in a boxing
    match is actually signalling something much more profound.
As though a scarf can look like that.
As though I booked the room before Santa's helpers came.
As though the helicopter was too full of broad beans.
As though the five elements were Earth, Air, Fire, Vest, Water.
As though Sunday ended half an hour before it began.
As though The Magnificent 7 was actually a cake.
As though The Three Bears made bagpipes.
As though in a race between a Sundial, a Moondial and a Stardial,
    the Moondial would always win.
As though spiders understand austerity's subtle subtleties.
As though the throbbing veins in the forehead can predict global
    shifts in economic thinking.
As though a necklace, when eaten, can give you glowing eyes.
As though animals do not become extinct, just invisible.
As though the discarded balaclava is the start, not the end, of a
    fertility dance.
As though taxis are sovereign states with their own currency and
    laws.

Elegy, Eulogy, Eelegy

Who died, then? Words did. Heart failure
Spreading like a sudden stain across the straining
Chest; pins and needles in your arm. Literally.

Who died, then? Who are we remembering
In this little church with its windows so mucky
They're stained glass, with its font so old

It's indecipherable, with its door so wooden
You can't see its emotions, just hear them
Squeaking? Words. They died. *Food.*

That's a word. *Asylum.* That's a word. *Bank.*
That's a word. *Seeker.* That's a word. They died
Perhaps because we tried to force them together:

Asylum Bank. Food seeker. Food Asylum. Bank Seeker.
Words, you see: dead as breeze blocks. Slippery as eels.

Figs

He leans over to pick up the
Figs. I lean over to pick
Up the figs. You lean over

To pick up the figs. And Him,
Me, and You are the same man,
The same fingers lean

Ing over to pick up the figs.
At different cupboards
Of our lives, we're an I, a He

A You. But here's the thing,
Here's the *tingaling*, here's
The *waspy's sting*, here's

The *songyousing*:
The. Figs. Are. Always. Figs.
The POV remains the same.

Dress them up in rhyming
Slang if you wish, (*nice fish
Posh dish*) if you want.

But the fig remains a fig.
Me? I'm everybody.
But where does that leave

The verser trying to write
About figs? You see my dilemmer?

Language and Politics

...the illusion that language consists of things called words.
— David Bellos

So when Terry (pate gleam) from Speke
Says 'is she angry, la?' he's really saying Shangri La.
It's a *drive by shouting*. Listen: *Mock-Gloucs,*

Faux-Northants, Somerset-lite, Half-i-shire chat.
And when I'm lost and late in a rush to a West Mids
Station and I'm asking despairing directions

The man in the scarf really does tell me to turn left
At *Toys Yam We.* Okay, another tack: Alan and Marilyn
Bergman, lyricists, describe a line with too many S's in

As a *basket of snakes*. So when Cyril (wellies, vest)
Sings the wrong words of one of their great songs
He goes *Memories/misty waters flowing slowly/*

Through the canyons of my mind is he still singing
The Way We Were? Okay, another tack: on the radio
The man describing the Udinese-Arsenal match

Shouts *This is a terrifically open watch!* Okay, another
Tack: a man in a music shop says to his mate, who is
Carrying an umbrella even though it's a sunny day,

There's a huge amount of sound inside that piano.
All this tacking: my little language-yacht must be
In choppy choppy waters! My flowery language-carpet

Must be very loose to need all this hammering down!
So maybe we should leave it to the professionals. They
Know how talk should be talkytalked. '*I have made it*

Very clear…'Heck fire! He even *sounds* like a Prime Minister!
Q: what has he made clear? A: the window. The view is now
Sensational. Depending of course where you are standing.

Language and Politics 2: Maps and Dog Ventriloquism
Combined in the Same Tale

Here's a map Chris once drew me.
It was how to get from the centre of Stoke
To his school:
STOKE----------------------------SCHOOL
It was folded up, of course.

What's that, Lassie?
There's a fire in the old barn?
It's spreading, Lassie?

When, in 1972, I visited Lundy Island
I had to leap the last two feet
From the boat to the shore.

What's that. Lassie?
What did they shout?
Come on, green trousers, jump!
That's what the folk shouted.

What's that, Lassie?
Why are whiffs always faint?
Well, as they say, Lassie:
You campaign in limericks
But you govern in shopping lists.

Here's a map of how to get to Lundy Island
From the mainland:
MAINLAND---------green trousers---------LUNDY

Sudden stink of drains
Like cracked roses
Cooked too long in a bedsit.
Have you got planning permission
For those cantos, m' boy?

What's that, Lassie?
What does my wife say?
She says I've got the gift of the gab,
Lassie, but I prefer to think of
That little-known miracle when Christ
Jesus walked on Tomato Soup.

CHRIST--------soup--------STOKE SHORE

Language and Politics 3: Complexity and Simplicity, a Debate

NB: Please imagine me reading this aloud as I walk on stilts and and sport a pink
tutu and wear the mask of a prime minister. Any PM, except De Rouge of course.

Looky, was this squirrel
Too complex to understand?
Is the fact that I'm standing
Looking at it some kinda
Metaphor?

(Come into the greenhouse and 'say' a prayer and 'light' a candle.
Be careful of the fork. Ah, too late. Still, the candle throws
shadows on the glass of the greenhouse prettily. What year was it
that gardeners got the vote?
What's that you say? They haven't got it yet? And that's why they
spend so much time in the garden because there's nothing else they
can influence. Oh, really, that's
Too too too too sad.)

Here's a confession:
I don't speak English.
I can't speak English.
But I can write it.
In fact, I'm Finish. Not Finnish, Finish.
Okay then, let's look over the shoulder
Of this man on the train and see what he's writing
In his journal:

Apple trees by railway line: south. Grantham: two trees, small
green apples. On closer examination: conkers. 1 tree big red
apples by retail park. Do I miss some when I write others down?
Mainly close to stations. One tree near a level crossing south of
P/boro, bright green apples. Red apples near Stevenage 1 tree.
Bright red apples v close to Stevenage Station. 1 impaled on a
fence post.

So, I'm walking up the street in Mapplewell
And a man in braces comes out of a house and says
Hey, pillock, what day is it?
And I say *Thursday* even though of course it isn't.
And the man in braces says
Reyt and shouts into the house
Telld thi!

Yep, I know, the debate's un-resolved.

My Kidnapping

It began as a day so ordinary that if it was a shoe
It would have been an ordinary shoe; the kettle
Boiled boilingly and the steam hung in the kitchen
Like drapes in a play. Someone came up to the door
And didn't knock and burst in; you know those clowns
That burst through paper hoops in sad circuses
In places like Northamptonshire, Isle of Wight? Like that.

He said, through his mask, I HAVE COME TO KIDNAP YOU
AND TAKE YOU TO A WAREHOUSE. GIVE ME YOUR WRISTS.
Sellotaped up, I was bundled into the back of a family car
And driven at high speed through the former coalfield
That has been my home since I was born and before,
Recalling my mother running rather too quickly
For the bus to Great Houghton in late 1955. GET OUT

He said. Not always a former coalfield, of course.
This sellotape's right, I said. WHAT DO YOU EXPECT
He roared, THE MINIMUM WAGE? In the warehouse,
By the green hill that used to be a muckstack, people
Were running as fast as Alf Tupper as fast as Mo Farah
Carrying boxes to put in boxes to put in boxes to put
In boxes to put in crates to put in crates to put in wagons

To put on roads to put in houses. GET OVER THERE
AND START my kidnapper said, and I tried to explain
That I was a poety-man not a warehousey-man
And he said WHERE HAVE ALL THOSE BOOKS GOT YOU
NOW, EH, FATTY? WHERE HAVE ALL THOSE POLYSYLLABIC
WORDS GOT YOU NOW, CHUBSTER? ARE YOUR MOOBS
FULL OF LANGUAGE? NOW PICK N PACK, SLOB McSLOB!

And I realised that this was where, in my late 50s,
I'd ended up. I still believed, as I believed in 1987,
That profit is unpaid wages, but I picked up a packet
And packed that packet like all the unpaid interns
Around me. For a moment, I stood still and looked up

At the light coming through a tiny window
And my kidnapper yelled LOSER! LOSE THE GAZE!

PACK THE STUFF! He hesitated, waited a moment,
His face rippling in a grin that, if it had been a kind of bed,
Would have been a very uncomfortable bed in a damp
Bedsit at the edge of a town that used to make felt hats,
And said HEY, WORD-MOUNTAIN, ANY OF YOUR BOOOOOKS
IN HERE? YOU PACKING ANY OF YOUR BOOOOOOOKS?
And he said books in that way that people say books

When they try to emphasise what divides us, not what
Staples us together. I shook my head; ran, sellotaped, fast
As I could because I was late for the future. Damn it, I was
Late for the present. And that is the story of my kidnapping,
On a day so ordinary it could have been an egg-cup.
An ordinary egg-cup, not a novelty egg cup. The warehouse:
It's as big as a mind. As big as a mind. As big as a mind.

Norman Came to My House

1.
And said *Reyt, Ian. Av written a poem.*
Can ah show thi it? It dun't rhyme

An it's abart me thowts. Me thowts abart
England. An it were reyt ard not ter mek it rhyme

Burra think a managed it. Modern poem, tha sees.
They dun't ev ter rhyme, do thi? Modern poetry.

Ah'll leave it wi thi.

2.

Later, I rang Norman to talk to him about his poem.

His answering machine was Norman with a phone voice:
The score is Barnsley six, Manchester United nil
And the second half is about to start.
So you'll understand that I can't get to the phone right now.
It's okay Norman. I'll ring back later, to talk about Modern Poetry.

Oboe

Brian took up the oboe at Paisley Grammar School. That and his love of
swimming perhaps accounted for his extraordinary lung capacity.
– Obituary of Brian Ball in *The Guardian* by Ian MacWhirter, 3/12/13

On any day, any early stroll or late walk
I get the coat and finger the pocket, stick
The finger right in, all the way in
To find the inhaler's comforting architecture;

Blue silo with your helpful cloud, unchanging
As a photograph of an owl or a teabag's satisfying
Shape as it absorbs the water, alchemises
The nowt into the summat that sustains.

I don't need it at all; I just want it there,
Want the contours of it to run my fingers over
And that little blue cap to take on and off
Like a boy in a folk tale might, in the evening.

Of course one day the owl might die, one day
You might run out of teabags. Until then, inhaler,
Let me touch you with my chubby hands
And play you like a lost medieval instrument.

Pumped; to be Accompanied by Pumping Music

I'm ready now with the words;
They're pumped and bulging, they hurt
A bit but that's good. They're ready

For the clashing and the groaning noise
They'll make when I jam them
Hard and fast and pumped, against other

Pumped words, veins bulging, eyes popping.
Now I'm ready to start! Hit the music!
Make it louder! What exactly is pumping?

Tell me?

Railway Ballad: Broken Rail

Most stamped up and down Edale station,
Breath visible. I stayed on the train,
I wanted to keep warm. I'd gone part way home
Then we reversed all the way back.
Just me and a woman who *had* to get to Lincoln.

Phones had been passed hand-to-hand,
Brief messages. Haunted and shaky requests
And a bag of mints opened and given out.
My trip, no, my 'journey'
Would now have its own deep past,

Its own Dark Store from where memories
Could be click and collected, could be bought
And then shipped. Hart Crane, John Berryman,
Can you lend me some insights ?
We're passing through Stockport, you see.

Lonnie Donegan? Anybody?
REMEMBER WHEN BOOKING A TABLE IN A
RESTAURANT SEEMED SO GROWN UP AND
SOPHISTICATED?

And a half bottle
Of Mateus Rose please.

A lawn is a simple cultural interface,
A blackbird walking on it
Trying to remember something:
How to fly.

Will tha want egg
Or pineapple wi thi
gammon?

And that bird bath, the one
That reflects the afternoon,
Reflects that plane defining the sky,
Those clouds telling the same story
With variations.

Ah prefer mashed
To rooast.

That path
That leads
Straight to the shed
With no messing about,
No wooden messing about.

Her dog
Knows every word yer say.
Every word.

The hedge
That catches the light
And saves it for later.

Tha looks
Reyt nice
In that
Green dress.

Someone has lit a bonfire somewhere;
Smoke is wandering down the street,
Hanging about, floating,
Hard to remember where it goes,
So hard to remember.
So hard to remember the smoke.
Where it goes.

Rhapsody, in a Jumpy Way, on the Word 'Unravel'

As a word, it does, endlessly, what it says on the tin.
The ghost word 'travel' hangs around on its platform,
Shivering; the composer Ravel turns the word
Into a moment in a French café (cliché, *je* know)

When a piece is abandoned, manuscript paper
Screwed up and chucked on the floor. An echo
Of 'unruffled' doesn't hold the word's horse in place,
I'm afraid. It's ruffled. I'm afraid. Horse is bolting.

In the 16th century the Dutch called a frayed thread
A *rafel*. I'm un*rafel*ling the word like a flippin'
Time Lord. William Hartnell talking to Ian the teacher
Outside Coal Hill School in that first episode of Dr Who,

The one I watched from behind my fingers. I couldn't,
Wouldn't, believe that Time could, ahem, unravel
Like that. That's what scared me. Not the Daleks or
The Cyberchaps. Now Time's unravelling. Feels

Like the 1980s round here. Winders brokk. Kidz hanging
Abart. Nowt apnin. Robots saying *Exterminate* to owt
They can find. The shadow of the word *unrivalled* is thrown
By *unravelled*. You ain't seen nothing yet, as Ravel said

That time in that café (cliché, *je* know) when he sat down
And banged out his Bolero. That insistent music
UnRavelling slowly, building up to some kind of climax
Then another climax and then everything is

In a state of *unravel*. Feels unreal, I know. Feels
Like something's been set in motion that can't be stopped,
Looks bigger inside than outside like t'Tardis
And I'm afraid that it won't stop unravelling.

The Indoor Glider: a Miniature

Shadow of wings
Falls over settee
So this isn't a hut
Or a tent. This be
A suburban home.

I'm the pilot
Swooping over this
Domestic scene. In
My head of course
Not in 'real life'.

The New Punctuation

a demi-colon is a pause in a sentence as light as a breath on your
neck a full-sto takes a sentence and seems to suspend it in the
air letting it down slowly a comma/comma makes you laugh no
matter how tragic the sentence a question Geoff gives the question
you ask a kind of music a fool stoop bends a sentence like you
might bend a snake to get it off your neck a colonnnnnn is heavy
and seems to make a sentence drag and finally stutter to a stuttery
end

We're Doing the Quick Crossword

Slowly. *Violent disorder. Riot,
Ruckus, rampage.* Outside,

A slow motorcycle slows,
Stops. *I've got summat O*

*Summat summat, T,
Summat.* My brow

Wrinkles until it looks older
Than almost every other

Part of me. Violent disorder.
Summat O, summat summat

T, summat. How difficult
Can language be? The motorbike

Accelerates away, slowly.
Of course we're both

Looking at different clues,
Of course we are. Silence

Hangs in the evening waiting
For the motorbike. *Ruckus.*

An Old Map

He knew the town like a taxi driver knows a town:
The short cuts through builders' yards, pub car parks,
Works Unit Only sliproads, the footpath
That's not really, the street so new, so unadopted
It never troubled SatNav for a light or a reference.

His favourite hours were the ones that felt unofficial;
The ones where late squeezed into early, diary-turners,
REM sleep-states when his watch ticked so loudly
He raised his finger to his lips and went SHHH
And a dog walker looked up, winked a rusty wink.

At that wicker time the poems came, or they seemed to:
Words scribbled like soup-stains on a Paperchase notebook,
Phrases seemingly overheard on the wings of an owl,
An insight from the lit face of a copper in a slow car.
What is literature? They ask. It is this. Biro click. Biro click.

The next morning he read them. Then he put them aside;
They were just the same thing over and over. A Style,
If you like. A template of a way of passing the time,
Of tidying the word-hoard. Standing up, sitting down,
Standing up, sitting down. Again and again: like a Vine.

New & Uncollected Poems

From 'Grafters': An Exhibition of Photographs of Working Life at The People's History Museum Manchester By Ian Beesley

A Group of Group Portrait Questions

Who is this awkward family of half-strangers?
What sport do these exhausted team-mates play?
Who left these dolls at the corner of the playroom?
Where has this raggedy army marched from?
Who asked them to stand so still, so still?
Why do they stare so, without blinking at all?
Who has carved these figures from skin and bone?
When will they be allowed to move away?
Who is this chorus from a terrible, forgotten musical?
How do they know we are staring at them from the future?
Who will remember their names and tell their stories?

A Light Breeze Carries the Stink into My Back Yard

Smokescape, Chimneyscape,
Pitscape, Brickscape,
Snap-tin-in-the-darkscape
A light breeze

Windowscape, Machinescape,
Muckscape, Kidscape
Chair-by-the-doorscape
Carries the stink

Earlyscape, shiverscape,
Heatscape, latescape
Bike-down-the-streetscape
Into my back yard

Epicscape, scalescape,
Rainscape, mistscape
Tiny-figure-by-the-wallscape
And there is no escape.

Glimpse

A sideways glance at how it really is;
A lifting up of artifice's long coat
To show the cheap clothing underneath
It was all we could afford

The steady gaze of the brand new camera
Unblinking at the mate you sweat with
Paying attention to the long ignored
It was all we could afford

Kept in biscuit tins and old shoeboxes,
Attention denied at the back of the shed
A way of life so casually hidden
It was all we could afford

How Small, How Very Far Away

You could be a full stop
At the end of a long sentence.

They told me I had to stand very still.

You could be a tiny stain
At the edge of a clean white shirt.

They said they chose me because I was little.

You could be a flower
Held up to the show the depth of the forest.

*They said not to worry about how I looked
Because the picture wasn't really of me.*

You could be a star
That gives us some idea
Of the vastness of the sky.

Can I move yet? My arms ache.

The Hero Explains

I said I needed to get home
But they said I had to wait
While they got the grey room ready,
Opened up the windows,
Made it lighter.

They made me take off my vest
And they gave me a new one
White as the moon.

I said you'd be worried
But they said I had to stand
And they raised my arm and said
'Keep it just there. Just there.'
In the air.

They made me drop my shovel,
And they gave me a new one
Light as a feather.

I said I was tired
But they said I was lying
And said heroes don't get tired.
I had to hold the shovel
Like I loved it,
Like I loved it.

Framed

Straight off the shift
And made to stand;
Look into this
Look straight at me
Hold this *whatever it is*
In your right hand
Look into this lens
We call it a lens
Stand still. Eyes open,
If you please. Open.
Look ahead. You are
A representative
Head still ringing
From the deafening hours
Of all your workmates.
We will frame you.

Do you comprehend?

Quartet

Here are four half-melted candles.
Here are four half-inflated balloons.
Here are four half-wise men,
Who know something the grafters don't.

Where are the people who made the table?
Where are the people who sewed the suits?
Where are the people who got the room ready?
Where are the people who polished the shoes?

Here are four half-baked loaves.
Here are four half-posed poses.
Here are four sets of half-rheumy eyes
Looking to a future the grafters will build.

He Finished Up Down Nine-Clog Pit

He started off apprenticed
To an older man with laugh-lines
Who taught him all the right ways
And took his time explaining
Till the young man got it right

Listen to what I have to say
As Monday limps to Saturday
Or you'll finish up down Nine Clog Pit

He grew into the workplace
Ate his sarnies in the corner
And the older man grew older
And took his time explaining
In the blinding shop floor light

Listen to what I have to say
As Monday limps to Saturday
Or you'll finish up at Debney's Dump

Learning piled on learning
Till he knew the ropes and wrinkles
Ate his sarnies in the corner
Could do the job like clockwork
From the clock-on to the hooter

Listen to what I have to say
As Monday limps to Saturday
Or you'll finish up with Black-top shakes.

And then he was the old man
With no-one left to talk to
To do the job like clockwork
Cos the jobs had all been outsourced
And the hours had all been zeroed

Listen to what I have to say
As Monday limps to Saturday
Or you'll finish up with broken dreams

And learning's not a lean-to
No, it can be a palace
But someone has to live there
Or knowledge ends-up homeless
Cos the jobs had all been outsourced

Listen to what I have to say
As Monday limps to Saturday
Or you'll finish up at Nine-Clog pit
Or you'll finish up in Debney's Dump
Or you'll finish up with Black-top shakes
Or you'll finish up with broken dreams

This Wooden Flag

This wooden flag
This wooden flag we all fly
This wooden flag we all wear

This wooden flag, craftsman built
This wooden flag will not flutter or flap
This wooden flag knows no borders

This wooden flag wraps us all
This wooden flag takes us home
This wooden flag will not tear

This wooden flag lowered to earth
This wooden flag lies underground
This wooden flag will rot away

This wooden flag
This wooden flag we all fly
This wooden flag we all wear

Cat Hills

FIRST HILL

Overlaid:
Palimpsest of a cat's
Claw

SECOND HILL

Here and   here
Atoms of Percival
Here

THIRD HILL

Sunset glint on
Sword's
Sun
Rise

FOURTH HILL

Rain
    Makes
        Cat hair
           Mud-raffia

Rhapsody on Boat Names and Some Observations on the Weather

Margaret, you carried Coal and Pitch
And the drizzle hung in the afternoon air
Soaking the heaviness of Pitch and Coal

The Stoat had a round stern, and the Hare
Had a round stern, and the Wolf had a round stern
But the Puma had a square stern.

William, you carried Coal, Sand and Nightsoil,
And the brief morning Sun made everything riper,
And the Nightsoil steamed, didn't it William?

Can you see the Cheetah sailing on the water?
Can you hear the Bison, can you hear the Beaver?
There is a menagerie waiting by the lock-gates.

Ellen and Ellen and Ellena and Emma
Four sisters carrying the wealth of the nation
As the fog holds them all like a fist.

Sun makes its way, rising and setting
As the water rises and settles. Sun in rain:
Glowing and soaking, soaking and glowing.

Doris was named after my sweet wife
Who could carry coal from one room to the other
And glide through the tunnel of the evening.

Ellen and Cheetah and Bison and Sun
Margaret and Ellena and Beaver
And Doris and Wolf and Hare.

From the Garden, with the Mushroom

What I recall is this; it was autumn,
And there had been an eclipse during which
I stood with my dad in the garden

And we watched as the street grew darker
Than it should have, than it ever did.
Now it was at least one day later

And my dad walked in with a mushroom
That had illustrated the lawn's green canvas
Since the eclipse turned the sky's tone

A dirty colour. He passed the mushroom over.
It felt like the skin of someone who lived
In a place where no light gleamed. Whatever

I write now, all these long years after
Can never describe the mushroom's scent
As I held it to my nose: earth and water,

And freshness, beauty. I held it to my lips
And bit it, much to my dad's horror.
It tasted like the stillness of a fading eclipse.

To Fold the Evening Star, January 1965

Street corner shop, lit by the glow
Of an overhead light
That could be left over from an idea
Someone had yesterday

Or so I thought,
Fair-haired angel of the evening.

Mr Kendall's glasses, lit by the hope
That the bus from Darfield main pit
Would give him a gaggle of blokes
Who would all want to buy matches

Or so he said,
Speaking silence with his glimmering eyes.

Coins in my hand, held in the heat
Of my ten-year-old mind.
I ask for a Star, in a voice
That cracks and breaks with fear

Or so I felt
Washing the dusk with silver

'Not a Mirror, young man?'
He asks, making a joke
As old as the moon. The bus
Slows by the shop, stops, wheezes

Or so it seemed:
It shut its sweet eyes with timely sleep.

I fold up the Star, holding it loose
In my child's gentle grip;
This star lasts longer
Lights my way home

Or so I sang
As the lion glared
Through the dun forest
That clung to the path
Lit by a paper, folded in two.

Notes & Acknowledgements

Grateful acknowledgement is made to smith|doorstop Books for permission to republish poems from *This Lake Used to be Frozen: Lamps* (2011), *Ah've Soiled Ma Breeks!* (2012), and *Jazz Peas* (2014).

Some of the poems in *Dad, the Donkey's on Fire* (Carcanet, 1994) were first published in *A Chin?* (Wide Skirt Press, 1991) and *More Poems Please, Waiter, and Quickly!* (Sow's Ear, 1988). 'The Inevitability of Snow' was written for a performance with the composer Luke Carver Goss and premiered at The King's Place in London in December 2010. 'Not a Real Bear but a Bear Nevertheless' was commissioned by *The Reader* magazine to mark the four hundredth anniversary of the first performance of *A Winter's Tale*. 'Dream of a Tree in a Spanish Graveyard' was commissioned by Adrian McNally and recorded with vocals by Becky Unthank. 'A Black Dog in Four Legs' was part of the Golden Fables choir project in Lincolnshire. 'Grisp the Wheel at Ten Past Two', 'There's Always a Man in a Cardigan', and 'What Happened to Freddie Galloway?' also appeared in *The Richard Matthewman Stories* (Pomona Books, 2009). 'Cat Hills' was written for a collaboration with artist Iain Nicholls. 'Rhapsody on Boat Names' was set to music by Ian Stephens. A number of the poems included here were set to music by Luke Carver Goss or formed part of exhibitions with photographer Ian Beesley.

Index of Titles